# Nostrad

*Other Aquarian books by J.H. Brennan:*

Dictionary of Mind, Body and Spirit
(with Eileen Campbell)
Discover Astral Projection
The Reincarnation Workbook
Understanding Reincarnation

# Nostradamus

## Visions of the Future

## J.H. Brennan

Aquarian/Thorsons

*An Imprint of* HarperCollins*Publishers*

The Aquarian Press
An Imprint of HarperCollins*Publishers*
77–85 Fulham Palace Road,
Hammersmith, London W6 8JB
1160 Battery Street,
San Francisco, California 94111–1213

Published by The Aquarian Press 1992
9  10  8

A catalogue record for this book
is available from the British Library

ISBN 1 85538 145 1

Typeset by Harper Phototypesetters Limited,
Northampton, England
Printed in Great Britain by
HarperCollinsManufacturing Glasgow

# Contents

Blessed is he that readeth, and they that hear the words of this prophecy, and keep those things which are written therein: for the time is at hand.

Revelation 1:3

## Incantation of Law Against Inept Critics

Let those who read these quatrains reflect maturely
Let the profane, the vulgar and the common herd be kept away
Let all – idiot astrologers, non-Christians – stay distant
Who does otherwise, let them be priest of the rite

Nostradamus 6:100

# Introduction

When Nostradamus died in 1556, he seemed at the height of his fame. He had been admired and consulted by royalty, his public following was enormous, and the uncanny accuracy of his predictions had many a noble glancing nervously over his shoulder. Yet the fame of Nostradamus in his own day was nothing compared to the fame he achieved after his death. For as events unfolded, it became plain that his *Centuries* contained a vision of the future stretching generation upon generation and embodying elements of such startling accuracy that even the most sceptical have found themselves persuaded.

It was not, however, an easy process, for while some of Nostradamus' prophecies are clear, many are not. The obscurity is deliberate. In the Preface to his *Centuries*, he describes how he decided to keep silent about certain of his visions for fear of controversy, but later decided to declare them 'in dark and abstruse sayings . . . under a cloudy figure'.

Fortunately, years of study have solved several of the puzzles Nostradamus habitually built into his verses and something close to rules of interpretation have evolved. These will not, unfortunately, unlock all his prophecies, but they do help.

The first thing to realize is that Nostradamus did not write his predictions in chronological order. Five quatrains referring to Napoleon, for example, are scattered between Centuries 4, 6, 7 and 8 with no hint of a link between them; and there are many other instances in which apparent references to the same event are even more widely separated.

The next difficulty is the language. Although the base form is medieval French, there is a sprinkling of Greek, Latin and other languages and dialects as well. Punctuation is, to say the least, eccentric . . . often nonexistent. Words, even whole phrases, have been dropped from many verses as being understood from the remaining context. All modern commentators reinsert them – or at least reinsert their guesses as to what they might be.

The next difficulty is style. Nostradamus may have been an excellent prophet, but he was an execrable writer and a worse poet. Even when he is trying to be clear, his text meanders infuriatingly. A letter to Henri II begins with these words:

> For that sovereign observation that I had, O most Christian and very victorious King, since that my face, long obscured with cloud, presented itself before the deity of your measureless Majesty, since that in that I have been perpetually dazzled, never failing to honour and worthily revere that day, when first before it, as before a singularly humane majesty, I presented myself.

What Henri may have made of the salutation is not recorded, but it is certainly guaranteed to bring a frown of concentration to modern brows.

As if it were not enough to be windy, Nostradamus liked to parade his education. Throughout his quatrains he tends to use the historical or classical equivalents of place names and even peoples. Thus France becomes Aquitaine, England Albany and the people of Savoy the Allobroges, an ancient tribe which occupied the region.

The final difficulty is coding. Nostradamus peppered his quatrains with codes of every description. He had a fondness for anagrams, so that 'Paris' might become rapis, and confused the issue further by gratuitously adding letters. Thus an innocent appearing noir (meaning 'black') might, by removing the 'n' become an anagram of 'king' (i.e. roi) and chyren, minus the 'c' stood for 'Henry'.

He would arbitrarily shorten the names of places and people, sometimes by a single letter, sometimes by more. Often the part stood for the whole, so that Paris might be taken to represent all of France. Heraldic and other symbolism is commonplace in his quatrains: the Russian bear, the Italian wolf, the crooked cross (swastika) and insignia from various coats of arms all appear. Finally, he was quite prepared to write phonetically, although this may be less of a deliberate coding as an attempt to make sense of difficult names, places or messages received clairaudiently.

But despite their obscurities, the sweep of his historical prophecies began to establish itself within a few years of his death and as the evidence built, the singular nature of his vision gradually emerged. In many ways, the vision was reflective of the man. Nostradamus was first and foremost a Frenchman, a nationalist and a royalist. He saw future history as if France were the fulcrum of the planet and could scarcely conceive of a world in which kings and queens were unimportant.

But for all the scholarly input, for all the psychological insights, for all the anagrams and puzzles solved, there remains one enormous difficulty in the interpretation of Nostradamus. Every interpreter, myself included, approaches the quatrains weighed down by his or her own prejudices.

This is particularly obvious when we discuss Nostradamus' vision of the end of the world. In modern times, it has become almost orthodox doctrine among Nostradamus interpreters that the prophet foresaw nuclear Armageddon obliterating the human race around the year 2000.

It is with some relief that I can report, quite categorically, he did not. Although several of his prophecies for modern times are almost as disturbing.

# 1
# The Attic Room

On the night of March 23, 1543 (or just possibly 1554 – the year is uncertain) a robed, bearded, dark-eyed man entered the topmost room of a modest house in the little French town of Salon de Provence and there began a ceremony so bizarre as to be almost incomprehensible to a modern observer.

It is likely that he locked the door. The Holy Office – official title of the Inquisition – had been established by Pope Gregory in 1231 and was fast approaching the peak of its power. It had long since added sorcery to the list of suitable subjects for inquiry, a list that already included heresy, blasphemy, sexual aberration and infanticide . . . and there is little doubt the robed man was about to attempt an act of sorcery. Besides, his parents were both Jews, although he himself had been brought up as a Roman Catholic. In neighbouring Spain, the Inquisition made a special target of Marranos (converts from Judaism). Who could say how far that disturbing trend might spread, especially when there was every danger he could be betrayed by his neighbours? 'Here where I reside,' he wrote later, 'I carry on my work among animals, barbarians, mortal enemies of learning and letters.'

The top floor of the little house had been converted into a study. It was packed with books. Some were on medicine and astrology – the two went hand in hand in those days. But there were many more on darker subjects: forbidden works like *De Mysteriis Egyptorum* by the Neo-Platonist Iamblichus, tomes of

alchemy and, most dangerous of all, Michael Psellus's fearsome
*De Demonibus* and that notorious grimoire *The Key of Solomon*,
a guide to the evocation of infernal spirits. [1]

There was also magical equipment. This consisted of a brass
tripod, a small lamp or candle (the flame of which provided the
only light in the room) a wand, probably of laurel, and a bowl
containing water. It is reasonably safe to assume that somewhere
in the chamber incense was burning.

The man in the attic room would have had no doubt about
the usefulness of this equipment. His reading of *De Mysteriis
Egyptorum* assured him that:

> Porphyrius says the art is not to be despised which, out of certain
> vapours due to fire under favourable stellar influences, forms the
> images of gods spontaneously appearing in the air, in a certain
> degree like the gods themselves, and possessing a very similar
> efficacy.

Elsewhere in the work, he could read a more sinister
interpretation of that term 'images of gods'. Here Iamblichus
states bluntly:

> For amongst the demons there is one who is chief and who
> exercises influence at the moment of birth and apportions to each
> his demon. After this there is present to each one his own guardian
> that develops a cultus [image] congruous to his nature and teaches
> him both his name and the most suitable form of invocation and
> this method is most congenial to the demons.

If the dark-eyed man was indeed working from *The Key of
Solomon*, he would have fasted for three days and abstained
from sexual activity for nine. Immediately before entering the
attic room, he would have immersed himself in sanctified water,
then intoned the prayer:

> O Lord Adonai, who hast formed me, Thy unworthy servant, in
> thine image, from plain earth: bless and sanctify this work, for the

cleansing of my soul and body, and may no deceit or stupidity be here. O Most Powerful God! Through whose power the people were able to walk through the Red Sea from Egypt: give me this grace, purified and cleansed by the water, pure in Thy presence!

This done, he would have dressed himself in white robes of linen or silk spun by a virgin girl and, ideally, worn at least once by a Catholic priest as he officiated at Mass. His shoes would also have been white as would the paper hat he placed upon his head. Every item of apparel would display those mystic symbols known to magicians as sigils. As he dressed, the man would have intoned:

Amor, Amator, Amides, Ideodaniach, Amor, Plaior, Amitor! By the powers of those sacred angels I dress myself in these powerful robes. And through them I will bring to a successful conclusion the things that I burn to accomplish: through Thee, O Most Holy Adonai, and Thy Kingdom and Rule is everlasting. Amen.

Once in the room, he would have taken a nine foot length of rope and used it to mark out a circle on the floor. Inside this circle a second circle would have been described, one foot less in diameter.

According to *The Key of Solomon*, such circles must then be fortified. This is accomplished by inscribing the Hebrew letter 'tau' at each point of the compass, then writing such Names of Power as JHVH, AHJH, ALVJN and ALH at specific points between the two circles. These should then be enclosed within a double square, aligned to the cardinal points. The outer angles of the squares are, in turn, cut by four further double circles, each a foot in diameter, fortified in their turn by the Names ADNI, AGLA, JH and AL.

If it all sounds like a great deal of trouble, it must be remembered that those using *The Key of Solomon* believed utterly in its promise that, once preparations were complete, 'then will the spirits appear and approach, from every side'.

Spirits – and particularly the infernal spirits conjured by these techniques – were not to be taken lightly.

The man in the attic room may not have gone so far. We do know, however, that he placed his laurel wand upon the tripod and wet his feet using the water in the bowl. Then, using the same water, he moistened the hem of his robe. These were simple enough actions, but they reflected something deep, ancient and mysterious: the pagan rite of Branchus carried out by the sibylline priestesses of classical Greece.

In Greek mythology, Branchus of Miletus was the human child of Apollo, the sun god, who had entered his mother through her mouth. As a youth, Branchus met up with his heavenly father while walking in the woods and, on kissing him, was endowed with the divine gift of prophecy. The Greeks established a Philesian Temple jointly dedicated to Branchus and Apollo at Didyma where, according to some analysts, madness and inspiration combined in the utterances of the god.

Ancient history records that the priests of the Branchus Temple betrayed its treasures to Xerxes, who looted the building, then fled (with the traitorous priests) to escape responsibility for his sacrilege. But the gods would not be mocked. The group settled near Sogdiana and died horribly in the sack of that city by Alexander the Great. The Milesians, meanwhile, rebuilt the Temple of Branchus to a scale of stadia so enormous that it became the largest religious building in all Greece – so large that it could not even be roofed.

What went on in that great temple was an almost exact duplication of the actions of the man in the attic room. According to Iamblichus:

> The prophetess of Branchus either sits upon a pillar or holds in her hand a rod bestowed by some deity, or moistens her feet or the hem of her garment with water, or inhales the vapour of water and by these means is filled with divine illumination and, having obtained the deity, she prophesies. By these practices, she adapts herself to the god, whom she receives from without.

In his mimicry of this ancient ceremonial, it is clear that our robed figure in the house at Salon was attempting to duplicate the feat of the Greek sibyl – he was, in other words, attempting to make contact with the god and, in doing so, to prophesy. One wonders what would be the consequence of such an operation? We know the results promised by Psellus in *De Demonibus* where he described a form of divination 'known and practised by the Assyrians' which used a basin and involved the 'coupling of demons with matter'. Psellus wrote:

> Thus those about to prophesy take a basin full of water which attracts the spirits moving stealthily in the depths. The basin then full of water seems in short to breathe as with sounds; it seems to me that the water was agitated with circular ripples as from some sound emitted below.
>
> Now this water diffused through the basin differs but little in kind from water out of the basin, but yet it much excels it from a virtue imparted on it by the charms which have rendered it more apt to receive the spirit of prophecy. For this description of spirit is tetchy and terrene and much under the influence of composite spells.
>
> When the water begins to lend itself as the vehicle of sound, the spirit also presently gives out a thin, reedy note but devoid of meaning; and close upon that, while the water is undulating, certain weak and peeping sounds whisper forth predictions of the future.

This sounds far-fetched. Yet the man in the attic room subsequently claimed to have accomplished much more than 'weak and peeping sounds'. According to his own writings, as he completed the ritual a voice sounded which filled him with such terror that his arms trembled. Then, out of the darkness strode the splendid figure of a god, who took his seat upon the tripod stool.

What are we to make of all this? The consensus of scientific opinion denies any literal results to magic. There are even contemporary magical practitioners – probably the most prestigious was the late Israel Regardie – who believe the ancient arts are actually a system of psychology, concerned, like psychoanalysis, with purely subjective forces and phenomena.

If this is so, then our robed man in the attic room had persuaded himself to hallucinate. In his magical madness, fuelled by an obsession with a pagan god, the contents of his subconscious erupted to overwhelm him and he stared sightlessly at visions as dazzling as those of any schizophrenic. Perhaps he burned narcotic plants along with the incense to aid the process, as many magicians have done before and since.

But appealing though this theory might be, it has a flaw. The flaw is that the weird little ceremony worked. Whether it summoned a god or any other spirit no-one can now know for sure, but for centuries there have been sober, intelligent, respected scholars prepared to swear that the robed man in the attic room did indeed develop the gift of prophecy – and to a degree unparalleled in human history. He was able, so they claim, to foresee events not merely in his own time, but for hundreds of years ahead . . . up to and including the present day.

It was a gift that made him famous long after July 2, 1566, the date he predicted (accurately) as the day of his death. His name was Michel de Nostredame. History knows him better as Nostradamus.

# 2
# Plague Doctor

Even without a gift for prophecy, Nostradamus would have
been a remarkable man. He was born on December 14, 1503,
at noon, according to one historian, at midnight, according to
another. [2] There is closer agreement about his background. At
one time he was commonly believed to have descended from an
astrologer/physician to the Royal Court, but it is now accepted
that his immediate forebears were of the small merchant class.
All the same, his background is worth investigation, since it
places his life and work in perspective.

Anti-semitism – irrational fear, loathing and oppression of
the Jewish people – is a fact of history. Persecution drove Jews
out of Babylonia and many took the trade routes to Spain and
hence the rest of Europe. In Spain they enjoyed a period of
relative peace, but the First Crusade revived the hatred against
them, catching those in France in the middle of the persecution
of the Albigensians.

Matters got much worse with the establishment of the
Spanish Inquisition in 1480. In Spain itself and, only to a
slightly lesser extent, in many other European countries, the
open profession and practice of Judaism became virtually
impossible. But there was one notable exception: the land of
Provence, in France, which for a time came under the rule of
the monarch French nursery rhymes still refer to as 'Good King
René'.

René of Anjou was, theoretically, King of Sicily and

Jerusalem, but may have found it easier to establish his titles as Duke of Lorraine and Count of Provence. Lorraine he ceded voluntarily to his son and Anjou itself, under duress, to Louis XI. In 1473 he established his Court in Provence.

Historically, the Jews of Provence had been treated a great deal better than they were in many other areas. An edict of 1454, for example, guaranteed them free practice of their religion. Under René, who was interested in the arts and any form of learning, Provence became something of a Jewish haven.

But René could not live forever. In fact he lived only seven years after his move to Provence, which then became part of the domain of the French Crown. Eight years later, in 1488, Charles VIII gave Jews a blunt and brutal choice: convert to Christianity or lose everything you own. The order was confirmed in 1501 by Louis XII.

It was at this time that Michel de Nostredame's grandparents were trying to survive in Provence. At some point during the period – certainly no later than 1501 – both maternal and paternal grandfathers, Jean de St Remy and Pierre de Nostredame, were baptised Roman Catholics. It scarcely needs remarking that this was a conversion of convenience: most Jews in Provence were doing the same thing. It also seems likely that both families continued to practise their Judaism in secret.

Pierre de Nostredame had a son named Jacques, and Jean de St Remy had a daughter named Renée. The families, who were apparently acquainted, decided the two could make a match. They were married and one result was little Michel.

The name chosen for the boy is interesting. In calling him after the Archangel Michael, Jacques and Renée de Nostredame ensured acceptability to both Christian and Jewish communities. Michel was never circumcised. Instead he was baptised in the Christian church and throughout his life he continued publicly to profess allegiance and devotion to that church. But there are certain indications in his early life that beneath it all, his loyalties may have been divided.

Jean de St Remy, young Michel's maternal grandfather, was a physician. Such a profession had profoundly different implications in the sixteenth century to those it has today. It meant, for example, that he was a herbalist: plant infusions were the only effective medicines known. It also meant that he was an astrologer. It was commonly believed – and taught in the universities – that the effectiveness of remedies varied with stellar influences at the time they were administered. Finally, almost certainly, it meant that he was interested in magic. For a Jew, such interest could only be translated into a study of the Holy Qabalah.

The Qabalah is a body of doctrines which form the mystical and magical heart of Judaism. Rabbinical tradition asserts it was first taught to Adam by the Archangel Gabriel and even the most sceptical modern scholars accept that it can date no later than the thirteenth century when it was finally written down. There is every indication that its roots are ancient. The name is derived from a Hebrew phrase meaning 'from mouth to ear' and suggests an oral tradition. Essene documents at the time of Josephus hint strongly that the tradition was alive then.

Scholarly analysis of the *schalscheleth hakabbâlâh*, the Chain of Tradition, indicates that it certainly reached back as far as first century Alexandria, an Egyptian city acknowledged as a world centre of learning. Philosophers in the city were attempting a synthesis of Arabian divination, Babylonian magic, Egyptian and Greek mythology, Platonic wisdom and Jewish Qabalah in one astounding system. Those who added Christianity to the mix were known as Gnostics. Those who did not were Neo-Platonists, the same Neo-Platonists whose writings Nostradamus is known to have studied.

But this is moving ahead of our story. In the days before young Michel de Nostredame had read anything worth noting, his maternal grandfather, the physician Jean de St Remy, decided to take charge of his education. The boy moved in to live with him.

In later years, Michel was to claim his grandfather taught him little more than mathematics, Greek, Latin, Hebrew and the humanities. But such claims may have been made with a weather eye cast for the Inquisition, for it is certain that he learned astrology as well and assisted in the preparation of infusions, the gathering of herbs and the compounding of ointments.

And while there is no written hint of it anywhere, it is equally certain that if Jean de St Remy was an initiate of the Qabalah, he would have taught that mystic wisdom to young Michel. It was Qabalistic tradition that the magical knowledge should be passed on to the eldest son of every generation. Michel was an eldest son. He had a younger brother who, deprived of the hermetic discipline, entered a career in politics and achieved notoriety by composing bawdy songs.

Jean de St Remy died while Michel was still a child and the boy moved back to live with his parents in St Remy-en-Crau where his education was taken over by his paternal grandfather, Pierre de Nostredame. He proved an exceptionally bright pupil and the decision was taken to send him to the University at Avignon. To gain entrance, he had to pass examinations in grammar, rhetoric and philosophy.

Grammar and rhetoric were largely a matter of memory and young Michel's memory was excellent, so he did well enough. It seems he did even better in philosophy – a subject which included astrology and natural science. The early work with his grandfather bore fruit and his examiners decided he was so far in advance of his fellow pupils that he was set to teaching them.

In later life, Nostradamus' secretary and disciple Jean-Aymes de Chavigny turned biographer to write *La Vie et le Testament de Michel Nostradamus*. In it Chavigny made the fascinating assertion that the young Michel taught that the earth was a sphere which moved yearly round the sun, as did the various planets. If this is true, it could be the first, scarcely noticed, example of his prophetic talent. At the time, learned opinion was unanimous in believing that a flat earth was the centre of the solar system. Galileo eventually propounded the idea of a heliocentric universe, but not for close on a century and even then he was persecuted for his pains.

As young Michel continued to do well at Avignon, his father Pierre decided the boy should become a doctor. Arrangements were made for a transfer to Montpellier, acknowledged as the finest medical school in the country. The reason for the school's reputation was macabre. It had since 1376 the right to dissect corpses and was entitled, once a year, to claim the body of an executed criminal. Repulsive though the system sounds, it worked. Montpellier professors built up over the years a knowledge of human anatomy far in advance of other centres of learning, most of which relied on ancient Greek and Roman texts full of superstition and guess-work.

This is not to say the curriculum of Montpellier would have met with the approval of modern medical practitioners – or even of modern patients. These were the days of the 'perpetual pill', a large pellet of metallic antimony swallowed to relieve constipation. Since the pellet had an irritant effect on the bowel, it worked well enough, but patients were encouraged to retrieve the pill from their chamber pots, wipe it off and set it aside for future use. Such pills were often handed down in families for generations.

The plain fact is that medical schools – even the best of them like Montpellier – taught a mixture of quackery, alchemy, astrology, magic, primitive surgery and, in all probability, a few efficacious cures. For three years, the young Nostradamus absorbed it all. [3]

In the Middle Ages, scholarly examinations were conducted by dispute. At the start of what we would now call his finals, he sat from 8am to noon, arguing points of medicine and logic with his professors. When the session finished, they were sufficiently impressed to award him the scarlet hooded robe which was the mark of a scholar.

But not the mark of a physician. To achieve that accolade, Nostradamus had to teach under supervision for three months, then present himself in turn to four different professors, each of whom questioned him relentlessly about the treatment and cure of a specific illness. This was followed, just over a week later, by a visit to the Chancellor who stuck a pin at random into a huge medical text in order to select the next disease for which the student was to prescribe. When Nostradamus managed all this, an aphorism of Hippocrates was selected – again at random – and he was required to prepare a thesis on it for delivery within twenty-four hours.

His professors formally disputed his thesis for four hours in the Chapel of St Michel which formed part of the church of Notre Dame des Tables. When the test was finished, it was declared a resounding success. A week later, Nostradamus received from the Bishop of Montpellier his licence to practise as a physician. Shortly after he qualified, plague swept through Provence.

Bubonic plague is actually a bacterium transmitted by fleas that have fed on infected rats. The plague bacteria multiply in the flea's digestive tract and eventually obstruct it. Then, when the flea feeds again, the obstruction causes ingested blood to be vomited back into the bite, along with the bacteria. The first signs of the illness arise suddenly and progress with alarming speed. Within hours, body temperature rises to about 40°C (104°F). The victim begins to vomit and experiences severe muscular pain and mental disorganization, quickly followed by delirium. Lymph nodes throughout the body become enlarged, agonizingly painful and filled with pus. Pneumonic plague is caused by the same bacterium but infection spreads through the inhalation of infected droplets from the lungs of a victim. This is the most contagious form of the disease and the form that progresses most rapidly. Even today, the infection will usually prove fatal if antibiotic treatment (streptomycin, chloramphenicol, and/or tetracycline) does not begin within 15 hours of first symptoms appearing. Left untreated, death usually occurs within three days in about 90% of cases. In the Middle Ages, it was not unknown for a man to wake in the morning feeling fine and end up as a swollen, pus-filled corpse by sunset.

In the fourteenth century, a single sweep of the Black Death, as bubonic plague was then called, wiped out about 75,000,000 people – almost half the total population of Europe – and established itself as the nightmare to end all nightmares in the collective psyche. The problem was, throughout the Middle Ages, that the Black Death never really went away. Although the continental epidemic was history in the days of Nostradamus, district and sometimes nationwide epidemics continued to occur. For the citizens of France and many other countries, plague sparked, died and flared like some demonic flame that could never quite be extinguished.

The situation was made worse by the fact that no-one knew how plague arose or how it spread. Germ theory lay a long way in the future. No-one suspected the importance of hygiene and sanitation. (In urban areas, the contents of chamber-pots were simply thrown out into the street, although it was customary to call a warning before doing so.) As a result, every new outbreak was met by superstitious terror, with many convinced that the disease was the visitation of an angry God. No-one was more terrified than the doctors whose job it was to end the nightmare: they knew better than most how horrifying the Black Death could be.

In the absence of any effective treatment or system of prevention, all sorts of weird ideas gained currency. One of these is commemorated in the nursery rhyme Ring o' Roses:

Ring o' ring o' roses
A pocketful of posies
A-tissue! A-tissue!
We all fall down

The 'pocketful of posies' in the second line refers to the fact that many people in the Middle Ages considered the 'noxious fume' of plague to be carried as a bad smell on the air. As a prophylactic, those who could afford it kept posies of flowers which they whipped out and pressed to their noses as they passed the white cross marking the door of a plague victim. That the posies were not particularly effective is attested by the final two lines of the rhyme. Sneezing was the first symptom of infection. Those who fell down, fell down dead.

Medical men were, if anything, worse than the general public. They used to soak their shirts in herbal juices, then stain them with multicoloured magical powders. Over this they garbed themselves in a sort of leather armour and spectacles, all to keep out 'tainted' air. Even then, they popped a clove of garlic into the mouth and tied a sponge across the face before they would venture near anyone with the disease. Their appearance must have been terrifying. It was certainly unwelcome for, with the inverted logic of the Middle Ages, many people blamed doctors for spreading the plague and stoned them on sight.

Whether Nostradamus dressed himself in this peculiar fashion is questionable. His ideas on how to deal with the terror that was sweeping the country were very different from those of his fellow physicians.

Nostradamus sought to cure the Black Death by means of 'rose pills'. We know exactly what was in them. Some four hundred dried rose petals were ground to a fine powder, then mixed with one ounce of sawdust from green cypress, six ounces of Iris of Florence, three ounces of cloves, three drams of odorated calamus and six drams of lignum aloes. The mixture was packed into lozenges which patients were required to keep under their tongues at all times without swallowing them.

One writer[4] suggests these may have been effective because they contained high concentrations of vitamin C. But it is rosehips, not rose petals, which provide this vitamin in quantity; and vitamins, even if present, are unlikely to have much influence on a raging bacterial infection. This is not, however, to imply that the pills were placebos. Herbal remedies have specific and often powerful properties. In concentration, they can produce results even where chemical drugs fail.

Nor was the Nostradamus formula randomly compounded.

Chinese herbalism, which draws on an empirical tradition dating back millennia, is recognised as the most advanced natural healing system in the world. According to the Barefoot Doctor's Manual issued by the Health Committee of Hunan Province, calamus is a detoxicant, aloes[5] would be administered in cases of vomiting and diarrhoea and cloves not only kill pain, but act as a disinfectant – almost exactly what would be needed to counter the worst symptoms of the plague.

But rose pills were only a part – and possibly not even the most important part – of a plague control system introduced by Nostradamus. He refused point blank to engage in bloodletting, the single most popular medical treatment of his age. He insisted on clean bedding and unpolluted water for his patients. He recommended moderate exercise and fresh air, well away from sources of infection. He urged a diet low in animal fat.

This system is fascinating. Within the context of his time, it was eccentric in the extreme. As a graduate of the foremost medical school of its day, Nostradamus would have been well trained in leeching (blood-letting) and heavily indoctrinated in its virtues. Why, so soon after his graduation, did he cast it aside? Clean bedding would have rid his patients and their families of the fleas which carried the infection. Clean water, for washing and drinking, would have promoted personal hygiene and helped stop secondary infections. The search for fresh air would have taken patients away from the focus of contagion. The avoidance of animal fat would indirectly prevent the consumption of the tainted meat – in particular the tainted pork – all too prevalent in medieval markets and on medieval tables. In short, the Nostradamus plague prescription included a hygiene regime of which any modern doctor might approve.

But how did Nostradamus develop such a system? There was no theoretical foundation for it in medieval medical thought. Nothing taught him at Montpellier would have set him on the right track, which may be why so few of his medical contemporaries attempted to adopt his methods despite the fact that they were so visibly successful. It is just possible that he might have stumbled accidentally on a single aspect of his system, but to imagine he might have stumbled on them all strains credulity. The question is whether it would strain credulity even more to suggest he might actually have foreseen the importance of hygiene in plague control.

# 3
# Nostradamus the Psychic

One day in later life, Nostradamus was seated outside his front door taking the air when the pretty daughter of a neighbour passed him on the way to the nearby forest to collect firewood.

'Bonjour, Monsieur de Nostredame,' she greeted him politely.

'Bonjour, fillette,' said Nostradamus.

An hour later, the girl returned with the firewood. 'Bonjour, Monsieur de Nostredame.'

'Bonjour, petite femme,' smiled Nostradamus slyly.

It does not, perhaps, take great insight to determine when a flushed girl has changed from child to young woman during a visit to the woods. But Nostradamus developed a reputation for psychism in his lifetime that was far more firmly based.

One night when he was closeted in his study, for example, a servant of the Beauveau family thundered on his door. Without waiting to learn the reason for this unexpected visit, Nostradamus opened an upstairs window and called down, 'You're making a great deal of noise over a lost dog. Go and look on the Orleans road – you'll find it there on its leash.'

The servant stared at him dumbfounded: he had in fact lost a valuable hound which had been left in his care. But after a moment he decided to take Nostradamus' advice and raced off to the Orleans road . . . where he found the dog. The story spread like wildfire and increased Nostradamus' prestige as much as, if not more than, his more sober predictions.

On another occasion while in Italy, Nostradamus was walking along a road near Ancona when he met up with a small group of Franciscan monks. He stood aside to let them pass, then suddenly flung himself at the feet of a young monk named Felice Peretti. The Franciscans asked him what on earth he thought he was doing and Nostradamus answered that he had to give way and kneel before 'His Holiness', a title normally reserved for the Pope. No-one was more surprised than the young monk himself, a former swineherd. The remainder of the party concluded Nostradamus must be joking, or mad. But in 1585, long after Nostradamus was dead, the ambitious Peretti, by now a Cardinal, was elevated to the papacy and took the name of Sextus V.

Aided by such incidents, the noted doctor's reputation for psychism grew so great that people sought to put it to the test. While he was a guest at Fains Castle in Lorraine, for example, the Seigneur de Florinville challenged him to predict the fate of two pigs they happened to be passing in the farmyard. Nostradamus told him the black pig would be eaten by the Seigneur himself, but the white one would be éaten by a wolf.

With that mischievous streak so often exhibited by sceptics, the lord promptly issued secret instructions to his cook that the white pig should be slaughtered and served that night at dinner. As the roast pork appeared at table, de Florinville remarked that no wolf was likely to get the white pig now since they were about to eat it. But Nostradamus shook his head and insisted it was the black pig they were about to eat.

The cook was called for testimony that would disprove the doctor. In considerable discomfort, the man explained that he had indeed begun to roast the white pig as ordered. But while his back was turned, a pet wolf cub belonging to some guards crept into the kitchens and dragged the carcass off the spit. Not wishing to disappoint his master, who had ordered pork for supper, the cook had promptly killed the black pig, roasted it and served it up instead.

Stories of this sort – the loss of a girl's virginity, the missing dog, the monk who became Pope, the pigs and the wolf – are colourful and entertaining. But do they add up to very much? We are being asked, after all, to accept the proposition that an obscure medieval physician was able to see the future. Could we not argue that he might have heard about the lost dog before Beauveau's servant arrived, that he knew the young Peretti had connections? And perhaps this was not the first time the wolf-cub had stolen something from the kitchens. If Nostradamus guessed it might happen again, had he not a 50/50 chance of being right about which pig would be taken?

Today, scientists refer to an ability to foresee the future as 'precognition' and have worked hard for decades in an attempt to establish its reality. Dr Helmut H.W. Schmidt, a German parapsychologist now working in Texas, developed fully automated ESP test machines, including radioactive random event generators. Routine use of computers to record results and hold data has become a further safeguard. And the bottom line has been that statistical evidence for the reality of precognition continues to emerge.

The laboratory work is supported by a mass of anecdotal evidence. In her analysis of thousands of testimonial letters received by the Parapsychology Laboratory at Duke University, Louisa E. Rhine estimated that reports of precognitive experiences ran as high as 40%.

Some of the anecdotal evidence is impressive. While she was Prime Minister of Israel, Golda Meir received a letter from a British housewife warning her of an impending attack by Arab forces and specifically mentioning the 'Heights of Golan'. The letter was postmarked October 2, 1973. On October 6, the Arab nations of Egypt and Syria launched a surprise attack on Israel and the Syrians took over the Golan Heights. The Israelis won the war with considerable efficiency,[6] but Golda Meir often wondered if she could have avoided the conflict altogether had the letter arrived before the attack began.

Charles Dickens was one of a number of distinguished individuals with personal experience of precognition. In 1863, he recorded a dream in which he saw a lady in a red shawl with her back to him. He thought he recognised her, but when she turned, he discovered he did not know her at all. She then introduced herself as 'Miss Napier'.

When Dickens awoke, he found himself puzzled by the dream because of its very inconsequentiality. The dream, though vivid, contained no dire warnings, no useful information of any sort, and he did not know any Miss Napier. But that evening, after one of his public readings, two friends came to see him . . . bringing with them the lady in the red shawl whom they introduced as Miss Napier.

Dreams of this sort are by no means rare. In 1927, the English aeronautic engineer John W. Dunne published a book called *An Experiment With Time* which described a whole series of precognitive dreams experienced by himself and others. Some of the dreams were of important, dramatic events, as when he foresaw a volcanic eruption in 1902 which swept away an entire town on the island of Martinique. But most were as inconsequential as Dickens' meeting with Miss Napier. One man reported dreaming that a group of people threw large numbers of lighted cigarettes towards him. Later he experienced the event symbolically predicted by the dream when a mechanical saw he was operating struck a nail embedded in a plank of wood and sent a shower of sparks towards his face. He was not injured, not even hurt. It is questionable if he was even particularly startled.

The vast majority of precognitive dreams seem to fall into this pattern. They refer to small, personal events of little importance and are far more commonplace than most people imagine. I even managed to have one myself, as a boy. It involved a school friend holding fireworks in a very unusual way. A few days later we went together to buy fireworks for the forthcoming Guy Fawkes night and my friend turned to me holding them exactly as he had done in the dream.

But the mundane nature of dream content should not detract from the extraordinary implications of such dreams themselves.

However inconsequential they may be as visions, they demonstrate conclusively that the future can be foreseen. If Dickens could do it and Dunne could do it and Golda Meir's anonymous British correspondent could do it, then it is by no means ridiculous to suggest that Nostradamus could do it.

The difference is that Nostradamus' predictions go well beyond a few inconsequential dreams. He was supposed to have the power to divine matters important to him – the manner of his own death, for example. A long time prior to the event, he predicted that close friends and relatives would find him 'completely dead near the bed and the bench'. His terminal illness began in June of 1556 with an attack of gout, a painful but seldom fatal complaint. He was confined to bed in his study, where he had a special bench constructed which he used to help him hobble round the room.

Towards the end of June, it became clear that gout was not the only problem troubling Nostradamus. He was exhibiting all the signs of dropsy, a far more serious complaint. On the night of July 1, his pupil Chavigny wished him good night and remarked that he would see him in the morning. Nostradamus told him soberly he would be dead before sunrise. When Chavigny led a part of friends and relatives into the upstairs room next morning, they found the body lying between the bed and the bench, exactly as predicted.

Nostradamus' personal concerns did not end with his death. Like the Pharaohs of Egypt, he was uneasy about the fate of his corpse. Once when a gang of louts attempted to harass him on the streets of Salon, he saw them off with the promise that they would never put their filthy feet on his throat while he was alive . . . or even after he was dead. He seems to have been obsessed by the thought that people might walk across the grave where his body lay, for he left strict instructions that he should be interred upright in the wall of the local Church of the Cordeliers. In a rather more public document, he gave this macabre warning to anyone who might consider the desecration of his grave:

> The man who opens the tomb when it is found
> And does not close it at once
> Will meet evil that no-one will be able to prove
> It might have been better if he had been a Breton or a
> Norman King!

His wife saw to it that his wishes were carried out and he was
indeed buried upright in the wall of the church. But his fame
grew following his death and rumours began to circulate that
a secret manuscript of great value had been buried with him.
In the year 1700, the municipal authorities of Salon decided
that the town's most famous son deserved a better class of wall
and voted to move the corpse.

They were aware of the warning about opening his tomb but
decided on careful consideration of his words that a quick peek
inside would do no harm, so long as they closed the coffin up
again immediately. So, in the year 1700, while the body was
being moved, the coffin was briefly opened. There was no
secret manuscript inside, but the skeletal remains of
Nostradamus were hung with a medallion the psychic had
draped around his neck the night he died. On the medallion,
starkly inscribed, was:

**1700**

It did not end there. In 1791, a contingent of national guards
arrived from Marseilles, drunk and looking for trouble. They
decided that the church in Salon might contain some useful
booty. Once inside, finding little of value, they thought to break
open Nostradamus' tomb: it was widely believed by this time
that anyone who dared drink blood from his skull would attain
his psychic powers.

There was an eight-foot stone slab protecting the coffin, but
the determined guardsmen, helped, it must be said, by several
of the local townspeople, smashed through it using picks. By
the time the Mayor of Salon arrived on the scene, the grave was

well and truly desecrated. Bones were scattered about the church and a guardsman, unwilling or unable to find blood, had filled the skull with wine.

The Mayor persuaded them to stop their antics by pointing out that Nostradamus had foretold the French Revolution, which was in full swing at the time. The guards gathered up the bones they had scattered and the Mayor had them reinterred next day.

But the reburial was not the only thing that happened on that date. The party of guards were ambushed by Royalists on their way back to Marseilles. The one who had drunk wine from the skull was shot.

# 4

# Nostradamus the Prophet

The line between precognition and prophecy is fine. *The Encyclopedia of Parapsychology and Psychical Research* has this to say on the subject:

> The only respect in which prophecy and precognition differ is that the former involves warning, consolation, or some moral or religious theme.

To which I would add time-scale. Precognition, as it is usually understood, tends to produce foreknowledge of (more or less) immediate events. Prophecy has a far longer lead-time. It also seems to me that prophecy is generally much more impersonal, dealing as it does with such large issues as wars, plagues and the fate of countries.

By the first of these criteria, Nostradamus' uncanny prediction of the year in which his tomb would be reopened could rank as a prophecy. But the strong personal element tempts me to classify it as a precognition ... and one Nostradamus turned into an impish joke.

Yet it is as a prophet, not a psychic, that Nostradamus is known to posterity. Even in his own lifetime, it was prophecy that brought him his most widespread fame. That aspect of his life really began in middle age when he largely abandoned medical practice to devote himself seriously to writing.

He left medicine at the height of his career. In 1544 he arrived in Marseilles to fight a new outbreak of plague there. Soon he was the most celebrated doctor in the city. Two years later, a deputation from Aix-en-Provence persuaded him to move to that beleaguered city so stricken by the disease that a majority of its citizens had fled, its parliament, courts and churches no longer functioned and weeds grew in the streets. The city gates had been shut for the greater part of a year to provide some sort of isolation. Nostradamus set to work and the plague, incredibly, started to abate. The city voted him a permanent pension and loaded him with gifts.

He was soon called to Lyons to combat the plague there. His work brought him into conflict with another doctor. Nostradamus insisted the city authorities choose between them. Predictably, the choice fell on Nostradamus, by now the most successful plague doctor in the country. The envious rival accused him of magical practice. The authorities ignored him. Nostradamus was getting results and nobody cared what methods he was using. In 1547, he returned to Salon loaded down with more gifts still.

At the height of his career Nostradamus was in his middle forties and, quite possibly, seeking a less hectic pace of life. His first wife had been dead for more than a decade and while he mourned her deeply, he obviously thought the time had come to settle down again. He proposed to a widow named Anne Ponsart Beaulme (née Gemelle) and she readily accepted. They were married on 11 November 1547.

Shortly afterwards, Nostradamus began work on the massive sweep of prophecies that were to guarantee his fame down the ages.

His first publication, in 1550, was an Almanac. It proved as immediately successful as his rose pills. The style was intriguing: he assigned a four-line predictive poem, or quatrain, to each month of the year. Such quatrains were to feature prominently in the more serious prophetic work he undertook later. For the moment, however, his Almanac attracted such attention that he was persuaded to turn it into an annual event and brought out a new edition every year until he died. It was around this time that he first met his future biographer, Chavigny. Chavigny had studied Greek under Jean Dorat, a huge admirer of Nostradamus, and now wished to study under Nostradamus himself. The physician accepted him as a pupil and began a relationship that was to last to his deathbed.

The year 1552 was a particularly busy one for Nostradamus. He brought out his Almanac and almost certainly continued work on his predictive *Centuries and Presages*. He also published his first full-length book, the *Traité des Fardemens*. It was not, disappointingly, a work of prophecy, but a recipe book of cosmetics, skin-creams, love potions and jam.

Three years later, he brought out the first edition of his *Centuries*.

The title did not refer to any period of time. Rather it described a collection of one hundred predictive quatrains, structured like those in his Almanac, but dealing with particular events rather than influences for a specific month. Nostradamus had been working on them for a long time, according to Chavigny, driven by intuitions of vast changes in Europe and civil war in France. His first edition, brought out by the Lyons printer Macé Bonhomme, contained three 'centuries' but, oddly enough, only just over half (53 quatrains) of a fourth. It was a long way from his final total – he eventually published almost a thousand predictions – but it brought him fame throughout Western Europe.

He seems to have expected something of the sort. According to Chavigny:

> He kept them [the prophecies] a long time without wishing to publish them, thinking that the novelty of the matter would not fail to arouse infinite detractions, calumnies and attacks more than

venomous, as indeed it fell out. In the end, vanquished by the desire which he had to be useful to the public, he published them; and immediately their noise and renown ran through the mouths of our compatriots and of strangers with the greatest wonder.

The instant appeal of the *Centuries* was actually quite surprising. Nostradamus wrote in a mixture of French, Greek, Latin and Italian. He used anagrams, initials and odd abbreviations. His syntax was terrible and the quatrains were a tangle without pattern or order. The result was an almost incomprehensible jumble. It still is, but we at least have the benefit of hindsight, which strongly suggests some of his predictions have come true. His first readers had no such assurance.

The obscurity of the work was deliberate. In a Preface, ostensibly written to his son César,[7] he spoke of his having used 'abstruse and twisted sentences' in order not to scandalize those who read his book. His vision of the future contained so much alien to the thinking of his day that he feared 'governors, sectaries and ecclesiastics' would condemn it out of hand. For that reason, he had decided to 'write down everything under a figure rather cloudy than plainly prophetic'.

This smacks a little of someone trying to hedge his bets and there are analysts today convinced that the bulk of Nostradamus' work is so obscure that it could be made to fit just about anything. All the same, those impressed by his predictions had not long to wait before the first of them was dramatically fulfilled. The 35th quatrain of his first Century read:

Le lion jeune le vieux surmontera
En champ bellique par singulier duelle:
Dans caige d'or les yeux lui crevera
Deux classes une, puis mouris, mort cruelle

This translates as:

The young lion will overcome the old one
In single combat on a field of battle:
In a golden cage his eyes will be pierced
Two wounds as one, followed by a cruel death

It has often been remarked that prophecies are easier to interpret after the event than before. If so, this one was certainly an exception. Word quickly began to circulate that the 'old lion' was King Henri II, who sometimes used a lion emblem on his shield. Before long England's Ambassador Throgmorton was writing to alert Queen Elizabeth I of speculation about the prophecy at the French Court.

Part of the reason for the ready identification lay with another prophet altogether, the Italian astrologer Luc Gauric. Gauric had told Catherine de Medici, Henri's wife and a woman fascinated by the occult, that her husband would become King and the beginning of his reign would be marked by a sensational duel. He then added that the King's life would be ended by a similar event. Henri did indeed become King and shortly after his accession the predicted duel actually occurred, a controversial match between Gui Chabot Jarnac and François Vivonne la Châtaigneraie. Henri attended the field at Saint Germain-en-Laye on June 16, 1547 and watched the death of Châtaigneraie.

A thoroughly worried Catherine insisted that Gauric provide the King with more details of the danger ahead. Gauric obligingly sent a Latin copy of the horoscope to Henri warning him to avoid all single combat in an enclosed space, especially on or near his 41st year. At that period of his life, said Gauric, he was in particular danger of a head wound which could result in blindness or even death.

Henri took the warning lightly. He commented, 'I care not if my death be in that manner more than in any other. I would even prefer it, to die by the hand of whomever he might be, so long as he be brave and valiant and that I kept my honour.'

Catherine, however, had read the first edition of the *Centuries* and obviously suspected that the 35th quatrain was confirmation of Gauric's dire prediction. She wrote at once to the Governor of Provence, asking him if he could persuade Nostradamus to come to Court which had, as was the custom, moved from Paris during the summer months to take up residence at St Germain-en-Laye. Nostradamus set out on July 14, 1556.

There was a brief meeting with the King, followed by a substantially longer one with Catherine who, we may be reasonably certain, questioned him about the prophetic quatrain that was already the talk of the Court. No record remains of their conversation, but he was sufficiently impressive to earn a gift of 130 écus from the royal couple. [8]

In June 1559, a dual wedding was announced. King Henri's daughter Marguerite was to marry the Duke of Savoy. Another daughter, Elizabeth, was to be wed (by proxy) to the King of Spain. [9] Henri ordered a three-day jousting tournament to celebrate. Thousands travelled from all over France to watch the spectacle. And spectacle it was, for the King himself had decided to take part. He wore full armour and a golden helmet. There was a lion rampant on his shield.

Catherine must have suppressed a shiver if she noticed a particular detail of the final bout. The King faced the Count de Montgomery, a captain of the Scottish Guards who was several years his junior and also had a lion rampant on his shield. Here, if ever, the 'young lion' and the 'old lion' were facing one another in single combat on a field of battle.

The official result of the joust was a draw. But then Henri, a competitive man, demanded a second bout. The captain tried to excuse himself – he may have been aware of the prophecies and noted the disturbing similarities of his present situation – but the King insisted.

So a second bout there was. The two riders thundered down the lists. Both made contact and, with a crack that silenced the crowd, de Montgomery's lance snapped and shattered. The splintered lance had penetrated Henri's golden visor. One lance splinter had pierced his throat. Another, sharp as any dagger, had skewered one eye and entered the brain. Henri was half blind and in agony from these 'two wounds as one'. Nothing his surgeons or physicians could do was able to make the slightest difference, and the King took ten days to die the 'cruel death' Nostradamus had foretold.

Nostradamus was given full credit for his prophecy. On the day of the King's death an angry mob stormed through the Paris suburbs to burn the prophet in effigy and call for his investigation by the Inquisition. He was accused not only of sorcery, but of secret Protestantism, which many saw as a great deal worse. It was not unusual for seers to be blamed for their visions. Gauric, the astrologer who had also prophesied danger for the King, once accurately foresaw the exile and death of Giovanni Bentivoglio of Bologna. The tyrant promptly ordered he be given five turns of the strappado, a hideously painful torture that dislocated both his shoulders and left him crippled for years.

Fortunately for Nostradamus, only the mob turned against him. Queen Catherine blamed de Montgomery for her husband's death. Although the dying Henri had ordered that no harm should come to the young Captain, de Montgomery decided to take no chances. He fled to England and, while there, became a Protestant.

Fifteen years later the Huguenots of Normandy staged a revolt. The Count de Montgomery, sympathetic with their cause and sensing personal advantage, returned to France and took charge of the embryonic revolution.

After a successful start to the campaign, his luck changed and he was surrounded by the army of the Maréchal de Matignon at the fortress of Domfront. Montgomery held out for a while, then negotiated a surrender that was at least to leave him his life. But he reckoned without the long memory of a vengeful Queen. She ordered six of her men to take him. On the night of May 27, 1574, they broke into his bed chamber and dragged him off naked under arrest.

Captain de Montgomery might have saved himself a lot of sorrow by a careful study of Nostradamus' *Centuries*, first published nearly twenty years before. And not just the famous quatrain about the King's death either. For in Century III, quatrain 30, Nostradamus had this to say:

> Celuy qu'en luitte & fer au faict bellique
> Aura porté plus grand que luy le prix,
> De nuict au lict six luy feront la pique,
> Nud, sand harnois, subit, sera surpris

> The man who struggled with a lance in a warlike deed
> And won his prize from one of higher rank than he,
> Will be surprised at night by six men
> Naked, without armour, [he will be] taken in his bed

It could scarcely have been a more apt description of what happened to de Montgomery had Nostradamus been present in the chamber.

But prophecies of de Montgomery's fate – Catherine ultimately had him executed – were not the immediate concern following King Henri's death. In the year that followed, Nostradamus' home was frequently stoned by Catholic mobs and at one point the threat of violence grew so extreme he was forced to take shelter with his family in the local jail.

Meanwhile the nobility were beginning to wonder about another of the quatrains, number 39 of the tenth Century, which read:

> The first son [of the] widow [shall make] a bad marriage.
> There will be no children [and] two lands shall be plunged into discord.
> Before the age of eighteen, while still a minor
> For the other, even younger [literally 'lower'] there will be a betrothal

The most important widow of the time was, of course, the
Queen (now Queen Regent) Catherine de Medici. Her first son
was Francis II whose unfortunate and childless marriage to
Scotland's Mary Stuart was predicted in another of the
quatrains:

> The unhappy marriage will be celebrated
> Amid great rejoicing, but will remain unhappy
> Mary and her mother-in-law will detest one another
> [When] Phybe [is] dead, the in-law shall be more piteous

Century 10, Quatrain 55

Erika Cheetham makes the ingenious suggestion[10] that 'Phybe',
an otherwise mysterious name, might be a typical Nostradamus
cypher in which the phonetic 'Ph' might stand for 'F' and 'be'
could indicate the Greek beta, or 'two'. Putting these together,
the result is 'F II' short for Francis II.[11] But even without the
name Francis, there are interesting and accurate aspects to the
quatrain. Certainly Mary and Catherine did heartily detest one
another, while the marriage itself was a disaster.

But what intrigued the French Court following the untimely
death of Henri was the third line of quatrain 39, Century 10,
'Before the age of eighteen, while still a minor'. A rumour
began to circulate that this meant the death of the young Francis
II before his eighteenth birthday. The fact that the boy had
always been sickly added fuel. Soon the rumour grew so
widespread that the Tuscany Ambassador felt compelled to
mention it to the Duke of Florence.

The suspicions of the Courtiers were well founded. Francis
did indeed die just six weeks short of his eighteenth birthday –
only three days after the Ambassador's letter was dispatched
to the Duke of Florence. Public reaction to the death was
graphically described in another letter, this time from the
Spanish Ambassador to his King, Philip II:

These catastrophes have struck the court with stupor, together with the warning of Nostradamus, who it would be better to punish than to allow to sell his prophecies, which lead to vain and superstitious beliefs.

But less dogmatic men than Ambassador Chantonnay soon had cause to wonder just how vain and superstitious the quatrains of Nostradamus actually were. There was certainly ample evidence to suggest he was well aware of the fate not just of King Henri II, but of the Valois dynasty as a whole. It was all there, in his quatrains and presages, for anyone with the wit to see it.

For the time immediately following Henri's freakish accident he wrote:

In the year when France is ruled by a one-eyed King
The Court will be greatly troubled
A great man from Blois will kill his friend
[Putting] the realm into difficulty and doubt

*Century 3, Quatrain 55*

For Queen Catherine, he predicted:

The lady [shall be] left alone in the kingdom
By the death of her only [husband] on a field of honour
Seven years she will express her grief weeping
Then [she will enjoy] a long life with good fortune for her realm

*Century 6, Quatrain 63*

About her seven children he wrote:

A coffin [shall be] placed in an iron cage
Where the King's seven children are held
The [spirits of their] ancestors will rise up from their graves
Sorrowing to see the fruit of their line dead

*Century 1, Quatrain 10*

Of Charles IX, he had this specifically to say:

> The savage King will exercise
> His bloody hand by fire[arms], sword and bow
> All his subjects will be frightened
> To see the greatest in the land hanging by their necks and feet

> Century 4, Quatrain 47

Dealing with François, who became Duke of Alencon, Henri III and Marguerite of Navarre, he wrote:

> From seven branches, they will be reduced to three
> The older ones will be surprised by death
> Two of them will be attracted by fratricide
> [But] the conspirators will die in their sleep

> Century 6, Quatrain 11

Henri III was dismissed in Presage 58:

> Le Roy-Roy n'estre,
> du Doux la pernicie . . .
> The double King will cease to be
> On account of the murder committed by Le Doux . . .

How did these various predictions turn out? All too accurately, as history shows. The one-eyed King was, of course, Henri II himself, blinded in the joust by the hapless de Montgomery. In the year that he reigned one-eyed – for ten days before the wound killed him – the Court was indeed greatly troubled; and not least by the prophecies of Nostradamus, as we can see from an examination of contemporary documents. The Venetian Ambassador Michieli, for example, wrote:

> Each courtier remembers the thirty-nineth quatrain of Century 10 of Nostradamus and comments upon it under his breath.

Since Blois was the royal residence, the 'great man from Blois' referred in context to Henri III. On May 12, 1588, an anti-royalist rebellion began in Paris and a revolutionary government was established loyal to the King's friend, the Duc de Guise. Later in the year, determined to rid himself of the pretender, Henri invited de Guise to his private apartments and, when he was foolish enough to accept, had him assassinated in the passageway. The following day the Cardinal de Guise, the Duke's brother, was also murdered. These vicious moves were far from popular either with the mass of people or with the aristocracy and certainly put the realm 'in difficulty and doubt.'

Queen Catherine, the 'lady left alone in the kingdom' never remarried, so Henri, who died on the field of honour, was her only husband. While it is unlikely that she was deeply enamoured with Henri (who spent at least as much time with his mistress as he did with his wife) she mourned him with the open formality that was the custom of the day. Then, in 1566, she put aside her widow's weeds – seven years after his death.

She herself enjoyed a reasonably long life – she died on the night of January 5, 1589, shortly before her 70th birthday[12] – although perhaps only someone as loyal as Nostradamus would describe her lifetime as one of good fortune for the kingdom.

Catherine had seven surviving children at the time of her husband's death. Nostradamus accurately predicted that they would be the last of the Valois line when he saw the final coffin placed behind the iron grille of the vault at St Denis which already held the rest of the ill-fated family. Their ancestors, he felt, must rise up like ghosts to mourn the fact that the dynasty itself had now died.

Charles IX certainly deserved Nostradamus' description of a 'savage King'. Indeed, there is every indication that he was more than half mad. While hunting he used an arquebus to kill every pig and donkey he met and took enormous enjoyment in beheading and disembowelling animals. Once he began to shoot randomly from a window of the Louvre in Paris, screaming 'Kill! Kill!'

Perhaps inevitably, this rampant lunacy ended in a national disaster. On the Feast of St Bartholomew (August 24) 1572, he sent orders to provincial governors throughout France to slaughter Huguenots, the beginning of an orgy of massacre and persecution that lasted until his death. While many were hanged by the neck during this ghastly period, a particular fact of the St Bartholomew massacre was that Admiral Coligny, one of the 'greatest in the land', was killed by the mob and hanged from a gibbet by his foot.

(Among the papers found in the study of Nostradamus immediately following his death were a number of unpublished prophecies in a form somewhat different from his famous quatrains. One of these 'sixains', as they were called, mentioned the Festival of St Bartholomew specifically, linking it with civil war throughout many cities and placing the blame firmly on Queen Catherine who, it is now recognised, profoundly influenced the young King in his murderous intent.)

The 'seven branches' mentioned in Century 6, quatrain 11, were, of course, Catherine's seven children. By 1575, all but three of them were dead. The survivors were François, Henri and Marguerite. Two of them, François and Henri, were 'attracted to fratricide' in one sense when they conspired to murder the de Guise brothers. They were similarly attracted in an even more personal sense when it seemed, for a time, that they were about to murder one another. Henri certainly accused François of plotting against his life and warned him such behaviour merited death. Nor was it an empty threat, for Henri tried to persuade his brother-in-law, Henri of Navarre, to orchestrate the 'disappearance' of François.

Despite all the scheming, both conspirators managed to die in their sleep, exactly as Nostradamus had predicted. But, again as predicted, they were surprised by death. François, a brutish young man who fancied his chances as a suitor of Queen Elizabeth I of England, was taken suddenly ill and died quickly. The sole remaining brother, Henri III, was called the double King by Nostradamus because he ruled Poland as well as

France. He was homosexual and was surprised by death when Jacques Clément, a Franciscan monk, assassinated him in his bed chamber. Interestingly, the word 'clément' in French is synonymous with the word 'doux' so that the description of the murderer as 'Le Doux' proved particularly apt.

The remaining child of Catherine, 'Little Margot', married Henri of Navarre, but despite rampant nymphomania remained childless to her death at age fifty-three, the last and vain hope for a continuation of the Valois line.

The prophecies quoted are by no means the only accurate predictions Nostradamus made about the royal family of his day. But they are enough to indicate his precognitive abilities were capable of ranging across the fate of others and well beyond the date of his own death.

Two questions naturally arise. How did he do it? And did his vision extend even further than the latest date (1610) we have so far examined? We shall tackle the first of those questions in our next chapter.

# 5
# Nostradamus the Astrologer

In the sixteenth century, everybody knew how Nostradamus made his predictions: he was skilled in the art of astrology. Nostradamus himself would not have argued. In a rambling dedication of his *Centuries* to King Henri II he stated that most of the prophecies had been 'composed and adjusted by astronomical calculation'.

Today, however, we cannot be so sure.

It would be difficult to find a competent modern astrophysicist willing to entertain the notion that the planets might have a causal influence on terrestrial events,[13] but the sheer persistence of astrological practice – it began in ancient Chaldea – has been enough to encourage scientific evaluation of its claims. To the forefront of this work has been Dr Michel Gauquelin, a French psychologist and statistician, whose findings in the field are worth examining in some detail. But to understand them, we need to know something of astrology itself.

Although the term is often used very loosely, a horoscope is strictly a diagram of planetary positions viewed from the place you were born at the time you were born. For convenience, the diagram is constructed as if the Earth were the centre of the solar system. Nostradamus would have believed this was literally true, although it is purely a convenience to modern astrologers.

In casting a horoscope, Nostradamus would have

incorporated into this diagram three major aids to interpretation – the zodiac, the houses and the aspects. The zodiac is a stylized representation of the fixed stars against whose background the planets move. The houses represent divisions of the circle which the planets appear to describe each day due to the rotation of the earth. The aspects are a series of angular relationships between planetary positions.

In one of his books, Dr Gauquelin likens zodiac, houses and aspects to cosmic roulette wheels around which the planets bounce like steel balls. Wrote Gauquelin:

> At birth each of the . . . moving balls becomes lodged in the mysterious slots of the three astrological wheels, which are intertwined one with the other. Thus the bets are placed. As the croupier of the cosmos, the astrologer records the position of each stellar ball in the sky at that moment. Then he pronounces his verdict, because, although we are unaware of it, our whole lives are preordained at birth. Have we won, or have we lost? The horoscope can tell us. [14]

There is actually quite a lot more to astrology than Dr Gauquelin's three 'roulette wheels', but it is probably fair to say that if the wheels are found to give inaccurate results, then the entire astrological system is thrown completely out of gear. So how did each fare under the rigorous examination to which Dr Gauquelin subjected them?

To test astrological ideas about the zodiac, he concentrated on the sign of Aries, which Nostradamus would have considered to influence an individual towards being 'Active and dominant, courageous, strong-willed, independent, pioneering, ambitious, energetic, restless, impulsive and hot tempered'. Since Arians are supposed to be strong in military matters, Gauquelin drew up horoscopes for 3,439 professional soldiers and calculated the frequency with which sun, moon and planets appeared in the various signs. He found that contrary to astrological expectation, there was no greater bias towards Aries in the sample than there was towards Cancer, which was supposed to predispose the individuals towards kindness, emotional upset and dormancy – characteristics hardly conducive to a successful military career.

Gauquelin went on to examine the distribution of the ascendant, an astrological term describing the degree of the zodiac rising over the eastern horizon at the time of the birth. According to astrologers, the ascendant is another important character influence. But in the charts examined, its distribution was exactly what would have been predicted not by the laws of astrology, but by the laws of chance.

Gauquelin then examined the charts of 16,000 celebrities in the fields of sport, science and literature. In no case were relevant zodiacal influences any more frequent than chance expectation.

In evaluating the houses, Gauquelin looked in particular at the tenth house, which according to traditional astrology governs professional success. Since the bulk of his studies involved the horoscopes of individuals who had been notably successful in their professions, he felt an examination of this house would be particularly significant.

His findings showed, however, that the 'scientific' planet Saturn appeared much less frequently in the tenth house for scientists than it did for artists. His sample actually showed a bias towards scientists being born when Saturn occupied the ninth house, indicative of, among other things, an interest in religion.

It did not end there. The sixth and twelfth houses tend to have negative associations in traditional astrology. The former is concerned mainly with health matters, while the latter used to be called 'the house of one's undoing'. Gauquelin discovered that if he were to construct a house interpretation on the basis of his case studies, he would actually have to reverse the traditional associations.

The aspects fared no better under Gauquelin's searching analysis. Try as he might, he could find no relationship whatsoever between the astrological doctrine of aspects and the reality of his database.

In one study, he decided to examine specifically those transits of Mars, Saturn and Uranus which astrologers believe to be so dangerous that they often predict the death of the subject. To do so, he compared the birth charts of seven thousand subjects with the planetary positions at the time of their death and analyzed the angles formed. This resulted in more than one hundred thousand specific coordinates. None of them bore out astrological doctrines.

Dr Gauquelin summarized his findings as follows:

In France we have been involved for several years in a systematic verification of astrological propositions . . . Our first task was to evaluate the statistical methods employed by the astrologers themselves. Their techniques were found to be severely limited: the laws of chance are ignored and conclusions are reached without support . . . the statistical laws of chance in every case superseded the purported laws of astrology.

Another step in our research was to calculate the horoscopes of more than fifty thousand people whose lives indicated some exceptional characteristic – a special aptitude, or gift, or stroke of luck – and also those whose lives were marred by exceptionally adverse conditions. For all these people we noted not only the day but also the hour of birth.

In no case did we find a statistically significant difference favouring the traditional laws of astrology . . .

Modern astrology, as a predictive method, relies on the survival of a hopelessly outdated view of the world and of life. It ignores the progress of astronomy and of human biology, as well as all the variables that affect behaviour through a lifetime. Every effort made by astrologers to defend their basic postulate . . . has failed. [15]

This is strong stuff, made all the more strong by the fact that Dr Gauquelin was a trained astrologer when he began his research and as such would have had every motive to establish its validity. His lack of bias is further underlined by an unexpected development. As a side-effect of his research, he was able to establish a definite statistical correlation between certain planetary positions in an individual horoscope and the occupation the individual was likely to take up. If, for example, you have Mars or Saturn rising in your horoscope, you are statistically more likely to become a famous doctor than someone without such an indication.

Gauquelin established several links of this sort and concluded that the planetary positions were not so much forecasting future career decisions as determining the development of specific personality characteristics. It was those characteristics which nudged the individual towards a particular career.

But Gauquelin has been careful to point out that none of this has anything to do with traditional astrology. The planetary alignments which showed up in his statistical analysis are not those which astrologers are trained to interpret. So far as Gauquelin is concerned, there is absolutely nothing to support their claims that their system works. Furthermore, his statistics clearly show it doesn't.

The great difficulty with all this is that it runs contrary to experience. If you take the trouble to have a horoscope cast by a competent astrologer, he or she will clearly demonstrate an ability a) to outline accurately your dominant personality characteristics and b) to indicate in broad terms (and sometimes in detailed particulars) the events of your life for years ahead. There is no question but that Nostradamus was a competent astrologer, able to use the art for insights into the future which kept his clients coming back for more. In 1564, for example, Queen Catherine (by then Queen Regent) proclaimed a two-year Royal Progression throughout the kingdom involving the entire royal family and a travelling court of eight hundred. The purpose of the 'progression' was public relations, an attempt to dampen religious unrest, but almost the first place it headed was the little town of Salon. There the adolescent King Charles IX rode in at the head of an entourage to summon Nostradamus personally to audience with his mother. When the prophet arrived, she promptly asked him to draw up a horoscope for Edward of Anjou.

This leaves us with a clear contradiction between observable reality and statistical analysis. There is no question about the accuracy of Gauquelin's figures, and the astrologers themselves have had every opportunity to criticise his method. So why is it that astrologers – Nostradamus in particular – have always seemed able to get results when astrology as a system can not?

There may be a clue in the recent development of computerized astrology. Once you have the necessary references, setting up a birth chart is not particularly difficult, but it does take time and effort. Since the work is largely a matter of mathematical calculation, it has long been a prime candidate for computerisation and following the spread of personal computers, there are now a great many programs on the market which will do the job in minutes. Professional astrologers have welcomed these programs with open arms.

But setting up a birth chart is only half the battle. The other half is assessing the result. This, too, can now be undertaken by computers. The program which calculates and prints the birth chart is simply linked to a database containing text interpretations of every possible planetary position and aspect. When the calculation is complete, the program selects the relevant texts and prints them sequentially to create the final interpretation. Theoretically, this should produce the perfect horoscope reading. It avoids all possibility of human error and absolutely guarantees consistency of interpretation. But while professional astrologers are generally delighted to use computer calculations, I have yet to meet one who considered computer interpretations to be anything better than a parlour game.

When you try to find out why, there is a tendency for the astrologer to stare into the middle distance and talk vaguely about nuances of interpretation, experience and skill. What quickly becomes plain is that astrology is not a science, but an art. There are good and bad astrologers just as there are good and bad musicians; and for much the same reason. The musical scale remains constant whoever is using it, but there are musicians who can turn it into a masterpiece, while others are able to transform it into nothing better than a mediocrity. The difference between the two is skill and that nebulous quality known as 'feeling'. In astrology, feeling is almost certainly another word for intuition.

Gauquelin remarked that his three astrological 'roulette wheels' interacted. Thus, to decide on the fundamental of a subject's personality, the competent professional astrologer has to consider 1) his sun sign, 2) his ascendant, 3) what planets appear in his first house, 4) the influences of the planets themselves and 5) his aspects. And each consideration is modified by the next, so that the final interpretation becomes a juggling act in which the astrologer makes a number of intuitive choices.

I doubt there are many astrologers who would disagree with this interpretation of the way they work, although one or two might prefer to substitute the word 'skill' for intuition. But I would like to go further. It has been my experience that there are some excellent astrologers who pay scant attention to the conservative traditional interpretations and use the whole jumble of astrological information as a sort of Rorshach Test into which they can project their visions of a subject's future.

This is by no means unusual. I have seen the same phenomenon in several others forms of divination including Rune, Tarot and I Ching readings. What we are talking about here is astrology used as a psychic uses a polished crystal – a focus for the attention which stimulates and channels an unconscious perception of the future.

As an astrologer, Nostradamus was only as good as his system . . . which, as Gauquelin has shown, cannot have been very good. Yet Nostradamus, even on the evidence of our limited investigation so far, managed to make extraordinarily accurate and detailed predictions for a number of important people. Consequently, Nostradamus must have gone beyond the rote interpretation of his astrological findings. He must, in short, have used intuition and/or psychism focussed through an astrological lens.

But, again on the basis of results, it seems Nostradamus was possessed of a gift far beyond that of any other psychic in history. If he channelled that gift through astrology, it is interesting to ask whether the gift itself was a natural, inborn talent or something consciously developed.

There is, in fact, substantial evidence to suggest the latter, as we shall see in our next chapter.

# 6

# Nostradamus the Magician

In 1560, the anxious Catherine de Medici, widowed by the ghastly accident at the tournament and uncertain about the fate of the Valois dynasty, summoned Nostradamus to the Chateau Chaumont and demanded further insights into the future. And this time Nostradamus did not consult the stars.

Instead he requested the use of a large room in which he would not be disturbed and there traced a magic circle on the floor, fortifying it with holy names of power and angelic sigils. Before it he set up a magic mirror, a black concave surface of polished steel, the corners of which were traced in pigeon's blood with the names YHVH, Elohim, Mitratron and Adonai.

At the stroke of midnight the Queen herself entered the dimly lit chamber, filled by this time with suffocating clouds of incense smoke. An old print shows her accompanied by two of her ladies in waiting, but it is far more likely that she came alone. What she and Nostradamus were about to do was blackest heresy and even a Queen could not afford to take the Inquisition lightly.

Nostradamus took Catherine by the hand and led her into the protection of the magic circle. Then he began an invocation to the angel Anael, a member of the celestial hierarchy supposed to grant prophetic visions. The focus of attention was the black mirror, in which the visions would appear.

There are similarities between this operation and the well-attested experiments of the Elizabethan astrologer/magus Dr

John Dee and his roguish Irish assistant Edward Kelley. Dee, for all his learning, had not a visionary bone in his body and was thus forced to hire psychics or mediums to describe the results of his magical operations. To do so, Kelley used a variety of devices, including a crystal 'shewstone' and a metal mirror.

But Nostradamus' art went beyond that of England's Court astrologer, for instead of a stirring in the depths of the mirror, it appeared as if a window opened in reality to give a panoramic glimpse of a 'room' beyond the room in which they stood. [16] In the room was Francis II, the Queen's son. He walked once around it, then abruptly vanished. Nostradamus interpreted this as the boy's impending death.

Another of the Queen's children appeared, the boy who would become Charles IX (and behead animals for amusement). He circled the room fourteen times, an indication, so Nostradamus predicted, that he would rule for fourteen years.

Then came the future Henri III, who walked around the room fifteen times, then Francois, Duke of Alencon, whose image was quickly transformed into that of Henry of Navarre, the man to whom Catherine was destined to marry her daughter Margot.

It was all depressingly accurate.

The description of the magical operation is taken from the work of John Hogue, [17] and it is only fair to say not all historians would accept the story as valid – or, if valid, as having involved Nostradamus. But for all that, there seems very little doubt that Nostradamus did believe in, study and practise magic; and that his prophetic abilities were stimulated by ritual practice.

He took considerable pains to hide his interest. In a Preface to his prophecies dedicated to his son César (just weeks old when the *Centuries* were first published), he voiced a warning couched in prose as purple as a horror novel:

I caution you against the seduction of a more than execrable magic, that has been denounced already by the sacred Scriptures, by the divine canons of the Church – though we have to exempt from this judgment Judicial Astrology . . .

Although many volumes have come before me which had laid hidden for many ages. But dreading what might happen in the future, after reading them I presented them to Vulcan, and as the fire kindled them, the flame, licking the air, shot forth an unaccustomed brightness, clearer than the light is of natural flame, resembling more the explosion of powder, casting a subtle illumination over the house as if the whole were wrapped in sudden conflagration.

So that at last you might not in the future be abused by searching for the perfect transformation, lunar of solar, or incorruptible metals hidden under the earth, or the sea, I reduced them to ashes.

But before the grimoires disappeared in that explosive flash of light, Nostradamus – as he readily admits – first read them. Clues to what he was reading are present in the last quoted paragraph. The 'perfect transformation, solar or lunar' was an alchemical goal, the transmutation of base metals into gold or silver. The 'search for incorruptible metals hidden under the earth or sea' was an even less savoury operation: it could be accomplished only with the aid of spirits, conjured by means of the blasphemous rituals in black books like the *Key of Solomon* or Faust's *Fourfold Harrowing of Hell*. For all his attempts to obscure the fact, Nostradamus did more than read the books. He conducted a deep study of occult philosophy, as attested by the liberal sprinkling of hermetic terminology throughout his prophecies. And with study came practice. The evidence is quite clear to those with a knowledge of the subject when they read the very first two of his published quatrains:

Seated alone in secret study
Alone it rests on the brazen tripod
A slender flame licks out of the solitude
Making possible that which would otherwise have been vain

Century 1, Quatrain 1

The wand in his hand is placed between the branches
He moistens the hem of his garment and his foot
Fear arises and a voice sets him trembling in his robes
In divine splendour, a god sits nearby

Century 1, Quatrain 2

The verses bring us full circle to the first chapter of this book where Nostradamus' most fundamental magical operation was described. This, as we have already seen, was reminiscent of the ancient practice at Branchus where the prophetess moistened her feet and the hem of her robe before divination. But if the methods were similar, can we be certain Nostradamus obtained similar results? Here again, the answer seems to be in the affirmative.

Iamblicus writes of the sibyl at Delphi that she:

. . . received the god in two forms – either by a subtle and fiery spirit, which burst forth upon any one through the crevice of some cavern, or else sitting on a brazen seat of four or three feet in the inner shrine, dedicated to the god, and where she was exposed on two sides to the divine influx, whence she was irradiate with a divine light.

Nostradamus too seems to have 'received the god in two forms' – and the same two as the Delphic seeress. The second quatrain, quoted above, indicates that he sometimes experienced the presence of the god in the form of a visible appearance which was accompanied by a glow of divine light.

In the Preface to his prophecies dedicated to César, he describes the second form when he speaks of 'certain persons to whom God Almighty may be pleased to reveal by imaginative impression some secrets of the future'. This is an extraordinarily interesting statement for, while Nostradamus goes on to speak about judicial astrology, he has already given the game away with his reference to 'imaginative impression'. The astrologer was engaged in more than sterile calculation. He was using his intuition . . . or some inbuilt psychic power. Nor is this speculation, for Nostradamus spells it out:

> . . . a certain power and volitional faculty came upon them, as a flame of fire appears.

The historian Charles A. Ward equates this flame with the descent of tongues of fire at Pentecost, as described in the Acts of the Apostles, but it is far more likely that the real inspiration was pagan. As Nostradamus told César:

> Perhaps, my son, I speak to thee here a little too occultly. But as to the hidden vaticinations which come to one by the subtle spirit of fire, or sometimes by the understanding disturbed contemplating the remotest stars . . . propheta dicitur hodie, olim vocabatur videns. [He who is called prophet now was once called seer.]

Later in the Preface he wrote of the way in which astronomic (i.e. astrological) calculation was overlaid by what he believed – or at least claimed – to be angelic inspiration in the form of apparitions.

One modern commentator[18] makes the ingenious suggestion that the legs of the brass tripod were 'angled at the same degree as the pyramids of Egypt in order to create a similar bio-electric force which it was believed would sharpen psychic powers'. Whether or not this was so, Nostradamus definitely used the ancient techniques of magic to sharpen his own psychic powers. Evidence also strongly suggests that, for all his protestations, he certainly did not confine himself to fasting, prayer and the supplication of angels.

One of the most obscure of all the Nostradamus verses is quatrain 42 of Century 1, which reads in the original French:

> Le dix Kalende d'Avril de faict Gothique
> Resuscité encor par gen malins
> Le feu estainct assemblé diabolique
> Cherchant les os du d'Amant & Pselin

One of the reasons for its obscurity, suggests Erika Cheetham,[19] is that the last line should read 'cherchant les os du Demon et Psellus'. Nostradamus, she believes, may have suppressed it to avoid an accusation of magical practice. If so, the accusation was all too justifiable. 'Gens malins', the 'evil people' is a term used to describe sorcerers. Thus the verse might be translated:

> On the 10th calend of April, according to the Gothic calculation
> Is revived again by sorcerers
> That fire which when extinguished results in the demonic gathering
> Seeking the bones of the demon described by Psellus

The reference to 'Gothic calculation' is pure prophecy. It refers to the changeover to the Gregorian calendar in 1582, after Nostradamus' death. The remainder of the quatrain, however, looks back to a description of demonic evocation to visible appearance in the works of Psellus.

Such evocations were by no means unknown in Nostradamus' day, despite the heady efforts of the Inquisition. One of the most detailed accounts of evocation – and its results – is contained in the private papers of Benvenuto Cellini, Italy's Renaissance master painter.

In 1533 or 1534, Cellini met with a Sicilian priest who was also a ritual magician. When Cellini remarked that he had always wanted to see a magical operation, the priest agreed to show him.

The site chosen was the Roman Coliseum. The equipment laid out included ceremonial robes, a wand, several grimoires, a pentacle,[20] incense, kindling and a supply of assafœtida grass, a plant used to dismiss demons.

The Sicilian drew circles on the Coliseum floor and fortified them by means of ceremonial. The priest began a lengthy ritual of evocation. An hour and a half later it bore fruit. According to Cellini's own account, the Coliseum was filled with 'several legions' of spirits. Cellini promptly asked them to bring him a young woman named Angelica, with whom he was in love, but the spirits ignored him.

The Sicilian undertook to perform the ceremony again in the hope of obtaining even more spectacular results. To this end, he made a fresh stipulation: he wanted a virgin boy to attend. Cellini brought a young servant with him, a 12-year-old named Cenci.

Much sooner than before, the Coliseum was packed with entities whom Cellini again asked to bring him his lady love. The spirits replied through the mouth of the magician that Cellini and she would be together within a month.

Although all seemed well at this point, the operation soon began to go wrong. The magician was the first to notice. There were, he said, too many spirits present – as many as a thousand times more than he had called. Worse, they had begun to misbehave. Twelve-year-old Cenci screamed that they were all being menaced by a million of the fiercest 'men' he had ever seen. Four fully armed giants were trying to enter the fortified circle.

The priest tried to send them all away. The little boy began to moan and buried his head between his knees. Assafœtida grass was eventually burned and the spirits began to depart 'in great fury'.

None of the experimenters felt like leaving the protection of their magic circle. They huddled together until morning when only a few spirits remained 'and these at a distance'. With the sound of Matins bells ringing in their ears, the sorry group left the circle and headed home, with little Cenci clinging desperately to Cellini and the Sicilian. Two spirits accompanied them, racing over the rooftops and along the road . . .

It is actually quite difficult to decide what was happening here; whether, that is, the conjured spirits were visible only to the inner vision of the participants or had some sort of objective reality. Éliphas Lévi, the French magician who managed an evocation of Apollonius of Tyana,[21] using a ritual drawn from the Magical Philosophy of Patricius, believed the 'wan form' which appeared was the result of a 'drunkenness of the imagination'. The Hermetic Order of the Golden Dawn, by contrast, used to insist that candidates aspiring to the grade of Theoricus Adeptus Minor perform a spirit evocation before witnesses. The spirit had to become visible at least to the consistency of steam.

But in fact, the objectivity of the entities is irrelevant to Nostradamus' magical practice. He had no desire to be brought a lover or impress examiners. What he wanted was the power of prophecy and an inward, archetypal stimulation of his psychical abilities would have brought him that gift as effectively as any demon. So whatever its essential nature, magic worked for Nostradamus. The rituals he embarked upon opened the floodgates of his vision and allowed him to peer with extraordinary clarity into the future. How far into the future we are about to find out.

# 7

# Visions of England

We have already examined the quatrains which charted the misfortunes of the Valois line. These are supported by others which provide a remarkably detailed picture of French history all the way through to Henri of Navarre's accession to the throne in 1594 and beyond.

It is impressive work, but hard going for those disinterested in French history. Yet while France was often uppermost in his mind, Nostradamus did manage to chart the future history of other lands as well. Among them was Britain; and what he had to say was fascinating.

At the time when Nostradamus penned his prophecies, England was a minor power on the edge of Europe with, objectively, little obvious potential for greatness. Yet the very last quatrain he wrote, Quatrain 100 of Century 10, said plainly:

A great empire is predicted for England
Powerful for more than three hundred years
Large forces of troops will move by land and sea
To the discomfort of the Portuguese

The Portuguese were one of the strongest maritime powers of Nostradamus' day, so that the prophet was obviously aware of the dynamic which would create the British Empire. Britain really became Great because of the skill and courage of her sailors and Nostradamus was well aware of this.

The time predicted as the extent of the Empire has caused controversy among commentators, some of whom argue Nostradamus got it wrong. There is little disagreement that the British Empire came to an end in the middle of the present century when virtually all dependent colonies won their freedom following World War II. Since the start of the Empire is usually set in the first Elizabethan era, this gives a period far closer to four hundred years than three hundred.

But are we correct in insisting that the Empire began with Elizabeth I? Certainly the piratical activities of British privateers laid the foundations of future sea power, but this is a long way from laying the foundations of Empire. As historian D.M.L. Farr points out, the real beginnings of Empire were rooted in the seventeenth century, not the sixteenth, and the platform on which it was built was the British colonisation of vast tracts of North America.

We tend to forget how important the American colonies were to Great Britain since they were lost in the American Revolution of 1776, but there is no doubt at all that they represented the original establishment of Empire. Although Raleigh and Gilbert gained a North American foothold by claiming Newfoundland in 1585, it was not until the war with Spain ended in 1604 that there was even the possibility of widespread colonial development for Britain. Large-scale settlement did not arise until the arrival of the Puritans in the 1630s.

If, as seems reasonable, this settlement is taken as the real beginnings of the British Empire and World War II marked its demise, then the period is indeed only a little 'more than three hundred years' exactly as Nostradamus predicted.

The Tudor monarchy which held sway in England in Nostradamus' own time gave way, in 1603, to the House of Stuart when James VI of Scotland gained the English throne. But it proved impossible to hold the two kingdoms together. The main problem was religious differences which exaggerated political divides. England was largely Anglican, Scotland predominantly Presbyterian and Ireland Catholic, except for the Scottish Presbyterian plantationers in the northeast.

There were also religious divisions within each country. In England, the most important movement was the Puritans, who wanted to establish a Presbyterian church. Although an overall minority, they had exceptional local strength in London and eventually won a narrow majority in the House of Commons.

By this time Charles I, who reigned from 1625 to 1649, was on the English throne. Conflict between his followers and the Puritans finally erupted in the English Civil War, actually two civil wars closely following one another. In the first, which raged from 1642 to 1646, the Puritans called in the Scottish Presbyterians to turn the tide. They already had superior economic, military and naval resources, but they were seriously divided among themselves. In 1648 the war was renewed, with the defeated King Charles now in alliance with the Scots. Charles was again defeated, and Cromwell's army, having seized control from Parliament, had him beheaded. For the next two years, the army subdued the royalists in Ireland. The Presbyterian Scots revolted and invaded England to restore the monarchy under Charles II. Cromwell fought back to defeat the Scots at Dunbar and Worcester. An enforced union was imposed between England and Scotland. England, Scotland, and Ireland then became a republic with Cromwell as Lord Protector.

Did Nostradamus foresee any of this? A close examination of his quatrains shows he predicted almost all of it, beginning with quatrain 70 of Century 3:

> Great Britain, which includes England
> Will be inundated as by a great flood
> The new league of Italy goes to war
> So that others band against them

Prior to the advent of James I, Great Britain did not exist. The political entity arose from the official unification of England and Scotland in 1604. But as Nostradamus predicted, the new state was quickly inundated by the mounting religio-political problems which eventually led to civil war. The 'new league of Italy' is sometimes taken to refer to the renewal of the Holy League in 1606, but since Rome, to Nostradamus, was the prime symbol of religion, he may have been hinting at the religious divides which were at the heart of the inundation.

Several quatrains refer to the life, death and times of Charles I whom Nostradamus, with his strong royalist sympathies, referred to sometimes as 'the great prince', sometimes as 'the just man'. Nostradamus plainly saw the fate of his royal successor, Charles II. He began his visions of this period of British history with the following quatrain:

> The great prince will be overtaken by divine ill-luck
> A short time before he takes a woman to wife
> His supporters and his credit will diminish
> Be advised: he will die for the shaven-headed ones

Century 1, Quatrain 88

Historians are satisfied that the real trouble between Charles and his Parliament dated from the time of his marriage to Henrietta Maria of France in 1625. Charles decided to disapprove of the Catholic persecution so prevalent at the time and actually decreed on his wedding day that it should cease. Parliament was, to put it mildly, unhappy with the edict and a train of events was set in motion which would end, as Nostradamus predicted, with the King's death.

> From the Kingdom of England an unworthy man is chased
> His counsellor will be burned in anger
> His followers will sink so low
> That the bastard will be half welcome

Century 3, Quatrain 80

This quatrain is unusual in that Nostradamus actually describes a king as 'unworthy', but there seems little doubt that he was referring to Charles whose undiplomatic behaviour was hardly worthy of a ruler. The counsellor who was burned was Archbishop Laud, following accusations of treachery in 1645. A year later, Charles' Scots followers actually sold him back to his parliamentary enemies, thus earning Nostradamus' accusation of sinking low. The 'bastard' mentioned in the final line was, of course, Oliver Cromwell, about whom the prophet wrote at least four quatrains:

> An ambitious colonel engages in intrigue
> And will seize the greatest army
> Then mount a false insurrection against his prince
> He will be found beneath his own flag

Century 4, Quatrain 62

Although Erika Cheetham points out reasonably[22] that this verse could quite easily apply to the notorious Colonel Gadaffi who overthrew Libya's King Idris in 1971, most commentators accept that it refers to Cromwell, who seized power within the army in order to oppose Charles I.

> By the shaven headed ones he will be seen to be wrongly elected
> Bowed down by a load he is unable to carry
> Such great rage and fury will he exhibit
> That to fire and blood all sex will be reduced

Century 5, Quatrain 60

The shaven-headed ones were the Roundheads who wore their hair substantially shorter than the more flamboyant Royalists. The Roundheads, as Nostradamus rightly noted, elected Cromwell (while the King ruled by divine right).

Nostradamus obviously disapproved utterly of Cromwell, as is clearly shown in the next quatrain we will examine, and considered him insufficient for his responsibilities. The final two lines of the quatrain are particularly interesting. Erika Cheetham, whose translation differs slightly from my own, considers that they relate to the fact that it was largely men (as opposed to women) who were killed in the 'fire and blood' of the civil war. While this is true, it is so common a truth in civil wars that one might wonder why Nostradamus bothered to mention it. My own translation allows a more subtle interpretation in that the Puritans sublimated their sexuality in violence.

> More a butcher than an English king
> While born in obscurity, he will achieve empire by force
> Without respect for religion or law he will bleed the realm
> His day approaches so closely that I sigh

> Century 8, Quatrain 76

The dislike Nostradamus felt for Cromwell shows clearly in this quatrain. Although he eventually ruled like a king, Nostradamus considered him more of a butcher because of the bloodshed of the Civil War. Although not a member of the aristocracy – the only sector of society whose right to rule Nostradamus recognized – he seized power by force. His lack of respect for religion arose from the fact that he was a Protestant. So far as Nostradamus was concerned, only Catholicism was worthy of respect.

Cromwell was born only one generation after Nostradamus' death: no wonder the prophet sighed.

> The great talker with limitless audacity
> Will be elected chief of the army
> At the force of his contention
> The city of the broken bridge will faint from fear

> Century 3, Quatrain 81

The 'great talker' again refers to Cromwell, who was no mean orator and, as Nostradamus says, was elected chief of the army. The final line is an ingenious example of the way Nostradamus coded his prophecies by classical allusions. The Latin for 'broken bridge' is pons fractus and the term seems to refer to the royalist stronghold of Pontefract which suffered two sieges during the Civil War.

> The fortress beside the Thames
> Will fall while a king is locked inside
> He will be seen near a bridge in his shirt
> Then barred within the fortress facing death
>
> Century 8, Quatrain 37

The fortress beside the Thames was Windsor Castle, which fell to the Parliamentarians when the King was defeated. Charles was taken there and incarcerated towards the end of 1648. He was held there for a month, then tried, convicted, dressed in a white shirt and beheaded.

> The just man will be put wrongfully to death
> Publicly and in their midst he will be slain
> So great a plague will arise here
> That his executioners will be forced to flee
>
> Century 9, Quatrain 11

> The great plague in the maritime city
> Will not cease until the death is avenged
> Of a just man condemned without crime
> The great lady is outraged by the hypocrisy
>
> Century 2, Quatrain 53

A royalist to the core, Nostradamus had little sympathy for Charles' Roundhead opponents and considered the King to be a just man who was wrongfully executed. A modern prophet might have stopped there, but Nostradamus was a child of his time and considered the person of the king (any king) embodied magical properties. These were the days when a royal touch was supposed to cure a variety of ailments and Nostradamus clearly believed that the execution of a king risked unleashing illness on his guilty subjects.

But if the connection was superstitious, the reality of the illness was not. Six years after Charles was beheaded, the Great Plague swept through London, killing thousands.

One wonders why Nostradamus virtually duplicated this prophecy, unless he was outraged at his first vision of the death of a king at the hands of his rebellious subjects.

> Ghent and Brussels march against Antwerp.
> The Parliament of London put their king to death
> The salt and the wine will oppose him
> On account of their actions the kingdom will be in disarray

> Century 9, Quatrain 49

Nostradamus returned to his theme, putting the execution of the King into context as war raged on the Continent. The 'salt and the wine' is almost certainly a religious allusion, underlying one of the fundamental causes of the Civil War. As the prophet predicted, the execution of the King achieved nothing and the kingdom was simply plunged into deeper turmoil.

A little more than two years after the death of his predecessor, the new monarch, Charles II, lost to Cromwell's forces at the Battle of Worcester. Nostradamus wrote:

> On the midnight hour, the army's leader
> Will run away, disappearing suddenly
> Seven years later, his fame undiminished
> Not once will yes be said to his return

> Century 10, Quatrain 4

Charles II did indeed 'run away' and 'disappear suddenly' – he fled in disguise to Scotland, thence to France. Cromwell was left in charge of the country, but his army dictatorship could not last. It rested on too small a minority, strained the nation's resources, and was bound to end with Cromwell himself. The restoration of the monarchy and Parliament was inevitable. Charles II was recalled from France and took the throne again in 1660 . . . after seven years of Cromwellian rule.

Staring across his vistas of the future from the attic of the little house in Salon, Nostradamus may still have rankled at the beheading of a king, for when he came to write Quatrain 51 of his second Century, he still insisted the 'blood of the just man' (i.e. Charles I) was on the hands of the Londoners who killed him . . . and that the plague which he had so accurately predicted was not enough to avenge him. Nostradamus foresaw another, even greater tragedy for England's capital city, and even spelled out plainly the year in which it would occur.

> The blood of the just man will be demanded from London
> Burned by fire in three times twenty and six
> The old lady will fall from her place on high
> And many of the same religion will be killed

The 'old lady' seems to have been a symbolic reference to St Paul's Cathedral, so that 'many others of the same religion' may mean other churches, or their congregations. What destroyed St Paul's? The Great Fire of London, which had the ironical side-effect of halting the Great Plague which had been raging for a year when fire broke out. Once again Nostradamus' prevision was deadly accurate. 'Three times twenty and six' adds up to 66. The Great Fire of London broke out in 1666.

And still the prophet had not finished with his prognostications of the British Empire. In one of his most intriguing quatrains he wrote:

> Seven changes will be seen within the British nation

Soaked in blood for two hundred and ninety years
France is untouched by Germany's influence
The Ram doubts the protector of Poland

Century 3, Quatrain 57

Some commentators have linked the seven changes with
changes in the royal bloodline:

1 Elizabeth I, from the House of Tudor, is the first example
of royal blood in this particular calculation.
2 Elizabeth gave way to the Stuart, James I, to bring in the
second royal blood.
3 The Stuart line gave way to Cromwell in the Civil War.
4 The Stuart Charles II regained the throne on the Restoration.
5 William III of Friesland took over from the Stuart line in
1688.
6 Queen Anne's ascension to the throne marked the return of
the House of Stuart in 1702.
7 The 'influence of Germany' appears in 1714 when George
I of the House of Hanover became King.

Historian James Laver interprets the quatrain rather more
subtly. He lists[23] the following fundamental changes which
occurred during the 290 years between 1500 and 1790:

1 In 1532, Henry VIII broke with Rome and proclaimed
himself supreme head of the Church in England.
2 Mary re-established the Catholic Church in 1553.
3 Elizabeth proscribed Catholicism in 1558.
4 A Commonwealth was established following the execution of
Charles I in 1649.
5 Monarchy was restored in 1660.
6 James II was dethroned by William III in 1689.
7 The Hanoverian dynasty replaced the Stuart in 1714.

The final line is often thought to refer to Hitler who was indeed as doubtful a 'protector of Poland' as Saddam Hussein was a protector of Kuwait.

Whichever interpretation of the changes one accepts, it seems somehow fitting to end Nostradamus' vision of the future of Britain with a rather less turbulent quatrain:

> The reign of the English
> Will bring peace and union.
> War itself will be held captive
> And for a long time peace will be maintained

As even the most cynical would admit, it is a very reasonable description of the Pax Britannica.

Although far more interested in his native land than any other, Nostradamus did make some attempt to follow the fortunes of Great Britain further. And as always, his fascination was for the ruling monarch. In Century 10, quatrain 40 he wrote:

> The young boy born to the Kingdom of Britain
> Which was passed on to him by his dying father
> Once he was dead, London disagreed
> And demanded the return of the realm from his son

Century 10, Quatrain 40

When a boy has a kingdom passed on to him by his father, he in turn becomes a king. But this king, although the rightful heir, found himself at odds with the capital authorities, who were soon demanding he give up his birthright. There is one British king whom this description fits perfectly – Edward VIII, the only British monarch ever to abdicate voluntarily. Edward succeeded his father, George V, in January, 1936. Soon after, he announced his intention to marry an American divorcee, Mrs Wallis Simpson. Mrs Simpson's status was even more controversial then than it would be, in the context of a royal marriage, today. The London Government, headed by Stanley Baldwin, refused to permit it and demanded that he abdicate ('return the realm') if he insisted on going ahead.

In a second quatrain, Nostradamus predicted what would happen next:

Since they did not wish to consent to the divorce
Which would afterwards be seen as unworthy
The King of the Islands will be forced to abdicate
And his place taken by another not marked out to be King

So it transpired. Edward announced his abdication in a radio address to the nation on December 11, 1936, insisting he was unable to shoulder his responsibilities without the help and support of the woman he loved. The throne went to his brother, George VI, who had not been in direct line. Edward was given the title Duke of Windsor and married Wallis Simpson on June 3, 1937. The happy couple left Britain to make their home quietly in France, the land of the prophet who had predicted their plight close on four centuries before either of them was born.

# 8

# Revolution Foreseen

The *Imago Mundi*, an early fifteenth-century manuscript housed in the Library of Douai contains this remarkable – and highly explicit – prophecy:

> Numerous great and astonishing alterations and transformations of the world, particularly as concerns the laws and the religious sects, will take place in the year 1789.

Pierre d'Ailly, author of the *Imago Mundi*, was not the only prophet to foresee remarkable events in 1789. The fifteenth-century astrologer and mathematician Pierre Turrel, a man so successful in his predictions that he was tried for sorcery by the Parliament of Dijon, also considered that year would be portentous:

> Let us speak of the marvellous conjunction which astrologers say occurs about the year one thousand seven hundred eighty and nine, with ten revolutions of Saturn, and moreover twenty-five years later will be the fourth and last station of the altitudinary firmament. All these things considered and calculated, the astrologers conclude that if the world lasts until then (which is known to God) very great and remarkable changes and alterations will be in the world, especially concerning sects and laws.

The *Liber Mirabilis*, penned by Jean Muller in 1476, comes within a year of highlighting the same momentous events:

A thousand years after the Virgin gave birth, when seven hundred more have passed, the eighty-eighth year will be astonishing and will bring in its train sad destinies . . . all the empires of the universe will be overthrown and everywhere there will be a great mourning.

Writing in 1549, a Canon of Langres, Richard Roussat stated:

Now I say that we are at the moment and we approach the future renovation of the world about two hundred and forty-three years, according to the general computation of the historiographers counting from the date of the compilation of the present treatise.

Adding 243 years to 1549 produces the year 1792, not the 1789 forecast in the other prophecies, but the events predicted were the same. For 1792 was the year of the inauguration of the revolutionary calendar in France. The year 1789 was the beginning of the French Revolution itself, an event of extraordinary importance not alone for France, but for the whole of Europe and, indeed, the world.

The Revolution took ten bloody years and violently transformed France from a monarchy into a modern nation in which power passed increasingly to the middle classes. Although there were a multiplicity of causes, political historians usually regard the weakness of the monarchy as a crucial factor. Nominally, Louis XVI, who ascended the throne in 1774, was an absolute ruler. In reality, he had almost no freedom of action. Attempts to tax landowners in order to pay for French involvement in the American Revolution led in 1788 to an Aristocratic Revolt, which itself became a trigger for further unrest. In 1789, the French Revolution proper began.

Its first phase was marked by extremes of violence. Political developments inspired a popular rising in Paris, marked by the storming of the Bastille on July 14. Revolts occurred in towns and cities throughout France. Peasants pillaged and burned the chateaux of the aristocracy.

The National Assembly established constitutional changes depriving the King of any legislative power except the right of veto. Louis' reluctance to sanction these decrees led to a second Parisian uprising. A mob marched to Versailles and forced him to capitulate. Louis and his Queen, Marie Antoinette, were moved immediately to Paris. France had become a constitutional monarchy, but the King was virtually a prisoner.

When Louis tried to escape from Paris, civil war seemed close, but the Assembly retained control. A crowd demanding a republic was dispersed by force and Louis was reinstated after he had accepted the completed Constitution of 1791. The Revolution was thought to be over and the National Assembly dissolved.

But within a year, the constitution collapsed. In April, the new Legislative Assembly declared war on Austria. Louis vetoed emergency measures and combined Austro-Prussian forces invaded. Insurrection broke out in Paris. On August 10 the palace was stormed, and Louis was imprisoned by a new revolutionary Commune. The invaders took Verdun, and alleged counterrevolutionaries were massacred in the prisons of Paris.

The National Convention established a Republic in September 1792 and sent their King to the guillotine four months later. The Convention had to contend with invasion, royalist civil war and widespread provincial revolts. When Toulon surrendered to the British, a demonstration in Paris compelled the Convention to establish the repressive regime known as the Terror. For a year France was plunged into deepest nightmare. A Revolutionary Tribunal sent state prisoners to the guillotine. Agents of the Convention enforced bloody repression throughout the country. A campaign of dechristianization, marked by a new Revolutionary Calendar, led to the closing of all churches on November 23, 1793.

From December 1793, when republican armies began to prevail, Maximilien Robespierre's efforts to create a united patriotic community became equated with the endless bloodshed. Finally, after a decisive military victory over the Austrians at Fleurus, Robespierre was overthrown and his deputies were guillotined.

As Dickens was to write reflectively in a later age, it was the worst of times.

Nostradamus wrote reflectively as well . . . centuries before. For almost two weeks following the storming of the Bastille, visitors to the fortress filed past a copy of his *Centuries*, open at a page which predicted the very events through which they were living. Nostradamus was obsessed by his vision of the Revolution and seems, in fact, to have decided on publication of his prophecies largely to warn of its coming. In the Preface dedicated to César, he quoted the biblical passage, 'Give not that which is holy unto the dogs, neither cast ye your pearls before swine, lest they trample them under their feet, and turn again and rend you',[24] to justify a decision to conceal his visions. But then he changed his mind 'in consideration of the vulgar advent'.

As his quatrains make abundantly clear, the 'vulgar advent' was the French Revolution.

Nostradamus seems to have been fascinated by the Revolution, its personalities and aftermath. One early commentator claimed that he devoted three quarters of his quatrains to it. While this is considerably overstated, he certainly did return to it again and again. It would be tortuous to quote every last quatrain and presage dealing with this great event, but a representative selection will be more than enough to establish that of all future events, Nostradamus saw this one most clearly . . . and was horrified by it.

The first hint of his concern comes in his letter to Henri II which, unlike his quatrain prophecies, contains a lengthy, rambling, but sequential picture of the future. Unfortunately it is a picture by no means easy to interpret – in most respects it is even more obscure than the worst of his quatrains – but the section dealing with the French Revolution is comprehensible and the dating clear:

Then there will be the commencement that will comprehend in itself what will long endure and in its first year there shall be a great persecution of the Christian Church, fiercer than that in Africa and this will burst out during the year one thousand seven hundred and ninety-two; they will think it to be a renovation of time.

In the sixteenth century, when Nostradamus wrote, the Vandals had only just ended almost a century of persecution of the Christian Church in Africa. With this historical event fresh in his mind, Nostradamus nonetheless foresaw the bloody campaign in his own country designed to wipe out the Church altogether. As a highly religious man, this would have marked for him the very nadir of the Revolution.

The year 1792, as we have already noted, saw the establishment of the new Revolutionary Calendar. As Nostradamus says, they thought this would be a renovation of the way in which time was measured.

That Nostradamus had a very detailed picture of the revolutionary process is shown elsewhere in his letter to King Henri when he states that the persecution of the clergy would last a little less than eleven years. If we take the earliest beginnings of the persecution as July 12, 1790, the day the Civil Constitution was adopted, and assume that it ended with the Concordat of July 15, 1801, the actual period of persecution is eleven years and three days. This might seem a reasonable enough margin of error for a man viewing events from a distance of more than two hundred years, but in fact we need make no excuses. In 1792, the adoption of the Revolutionary Calendar caused the 'disappearance' of nine days. When this is taken into account, it is clear that Nostradamus was absolutely correct in claiming the persecution would last 'a little less than eleven years'.

Although Nostradamus did not write his quatrains sequentially, it is perhaps significant that having discussed his methods of divination in the first two verses of his very first Century, he could no longer wait to pen his warning of the 'vulgar advent'. He wrote:

When the litter is overturned by the torrent
And their faces are hidden by their cloaks
The republic will be troubled by the revolutionaries
As both the Whites and the Reds will be equally mistaken

Century 1, Quatrain 3

Litters were, of course, one of the forms of transport favoured by the aristocracy and Nostradamus' picture of litters overturned by the mob is a vivid symbol of what happened during a Revolution in which members of the nobility were quickly forced into hiding.

It should be noted that he refers to France as a republic, a state of affairs virtually unthinkable in his own day. The original text of the third line of this quatrain reads, 'La république par gens nouveaux vexée'. I have translated 'gens nouveaux' (literally 'new people') as 'revolutionaries' since they would certainly have been a new breed to Nostradamus. His mention of the Whites and the Reds could not be more specific. White was the colour of the royalists, red the colour adopted by the revolutionaries.

Nostradamus returns again and again to the plight of the clergy during the Revolution and in Century 6, Quatrain 23, broadly outlines its entire sequence of events:

Ancient traditions, which served as ramparts, shall be denounced
And the people shall be set against their king
A brief truce is declared, then the holy laws become worse
Never was Paris in such a dreadful situation

During the Revolution, the old ways which had been the bulwark of society for centuries were indeed denounced and the people set against the monarchy. There was a brief truce in 1791, but then the whole thing flared again and the capital especially reached a critical point.

All this is impressive enough, but when writing of the French Revolution Nostradamus focussed on a wealth of specific detail that is almost beyond belief. Nowhere is this more evident than when he describes the famous Flight to Varennes. The historical facts of the flight will require some explanation here.

By the year 1792, King Louis XVI had become convinced that he and his unpopular Queen were captive in his own country, and he became obsessed by the idea of escape. Although he might have done so fairly easily on his own – and joined up with his troops at the frontier – the Queen made him promise not to leave without her and the children. Plans for the great escape took shape; and inept plans they were. They arranged to travel secretly in a berline, which is a huge private coach virtually guaranteed to attract attention, despite suggestions that two smaller coaches might be better.

The King decreed that their escape route should be through Varennes, even when warned that this route must arouse suspicion.

Then the King began to vacillate about the date of their departure. At first it was set for June 11, then postponed until June 19. Troop detachments were organized for various points along the route and men and fresh horses were to wait at Varennes. Then the King remembered he was not due to be paid from the Civil List until the morning of the 20th and promptly postponed everything again for twenty-four hours. The arrangements were thrown into disarray.

Against this background, things got worse. The men chosen to accompany the party were selected at random. None of them knew the route and one of them did not even know his way through Paris. Instead of dressing them inconspicuously, they were ordered to don the livery of the Prince de Condé who had already fled and whose servants were consequently under substantial suspicion.

Queen Marie Antoinette could not face the prospect of a journey without a suitable jewel box for her valuables and commissioned one specially from a team of Parisian jewellers. Marie Antoinette was to travel as 'Madame de Korff', and Louis was supposed to be her valet. She had chosen a white gown which befitted her supposed rank and he was inconspicuously dressed in grey. But old habits died hard and he climbed into the seat of the main coach opposite his supposed mistress. He also ordered that it be drawn by a team of six horses, a number specifically reserved for royalty.

If they were worried about attack, they did not show it. Firearms were packed away with the luggage and the footmen given only small hunting knives. Monsieur d'Agout had been recommended as their guide. He knew the way and had proven himself a steadfast individual. With a fine sense of decorum, the King took his children's governess instead: she outranked d'Agout in title.

There was an outrider, Monsieur de Choiseul, who was to go swiftly twelve hours before the royal party and prepare the way. As he was about to set off, the Queen insisted he take with him her hairdresser from whom she could not bear to be parted.

When the moment came to set off, they proceeded separately to the huge berline which awaited them at the Barrière de Clichy. Marie Antoinette and her attendant promptly got lost and had to ask the way. Placed on the right road again, they then contrived only just to miss being run over by Citizen Lafayette, who had only recently personally promised the Assembly that the royal family would never escape. Fortunately Lafayette, in this instance, proved as silly as his Queen and failed to notice whom he had nearly knocked down.

Thus the party set out and at Montmirail the first disaster struck when the axle of the coach broke and two hours were lost in repairs. It should have been an incentive for haste – the last-minute postponement meant they were already twenty-four hours late for their appointed meetings with the King's troops – but then Louis spotted a little hill that took his fancy and the party waited around for a further half hour while he climbed it.

With an instinct for secrecy that would have done justice to
a public relations expert, the King showed himself at Chalons
and was promptly recognized. As if to draw further attention
to the party, two of the horses fell down, slightly injuring a
postillion. When they finally set off again, a sympathetic
stranger called, 'Your plans are ill-conceived – you will be
arrested!' Truer words were seldom spoken.

The first contingent of the soldiers who would guarantee
their safety should have been waiting for them at Pont-de-
Somme-Vesle. But the men, having arrived a day earlier in
accordance with their instructions, had been driven away by the
threatening attitude of the townspeople. The royal party
proceeded unescorted to Sainte-Menehould where the King was
recognized by Postmaster Drouet, a former Deputy of the
Federation. Although Drouet provided them with fresh horses,
he also reported his discovery to the municipal authorities and
was told by them to give chase.

It was dark by the time the King arrived at Varennes, only
to find the expected relay of horses was missing. While the
party looked for it – the horses had, in fact, been left at the
other side of the town – Drouet caught up with them and
blocked the exit road by overturning a cart of furniture on a
narrow bridge. He then alerted Monsieur Saulce, the Procureur
of the Commune.

The King's party reached the centre of the town where the
horses of the great coach were seized and papers were
demanded. These were quickly produced and found to be in
order (as they had to be since they were signed by the King
himself) but by now crowds were pouring into Varennes alerted
by the news of the King's flight. Saulce insisted that the party
remain the night and Louis, with no real alternative, agreed.
By morning, a messenger had arrived from the National
Assembly. The King was ordered to return.

Varennes, if its citizens will forgive me for saying so, is a small
population centre with few claims to fame. Apart from Louis'
flight, it has never appeared in the history books and in all

probability never will. That such a place should be pinpointed in relation to the events of the French Revolution must lie far beyond the long arm of coincidence. Yet Nostradamus, writing two hundred and thirty years in advance of the event, had this to say:

> By night there will come by way of the forest of Reins
> A married couple arriving by a circuitous route
> One a Queen, stony white, the King in grey like a monk at Varennes
> An elected ruler. It shall result in tempest, fire and bloody slicing

> Century 9, Quatrain 20

There is, according to historian James Laver, only one mistake in this quatrain: no 'forest of Reins' appears on any map. The remainder, however, is all too accurate. Here we have a married couple, a King and Queen, who travelled to Varennes by a circuitous route. The Queen was dressed in a white gown (and one of her contemporaries records that following the incident at Varennes, her hair turned white) while the King was dressed in grey. Louis was indeed an elected King, the first in history, since prior to the Revolution, kings were believed to rule by divine right.

With a sure instinct for the dramatic, Nostradamus left his most striking – and horrifying – prophecy to the end. The result of the flight would be a storm of violence and blood. He even found the word trancher (slicing) to describe the monstrous machine he saw in his visions. It was, of course, the guillotine.

If this quatrain is not convincing enough, Nostradamus penned another on the same theme:

> The husband alone will receive the mitre
> Returning, conflict will sweep across the Tuileries

> By five hundred men a traitor will be given Narbonne's title
> And from Saulce we will have oil

Century 9, Quatrain 34

The 'husband alone' was Louis. Following his return from Varennes, the Tuileries palace was invaded by a mob which forced the King to wear the red cap of liberty, a headpiece which bears a striking resemblance to a bishop's mitre. History records a second invasion some two months later of exactly five hundred men. The Comte de Narbonne was the King's war minister, a title soon bestowed on a revolutionary. Saulce we have already met: he was the Procureur who stopped the King at Varennes. By trade he was a merchant and chandler. One of his staples was the sale of oil.

It goes without saying that had the King succeeded in his flight to Varennes, the history of the Revolution might have been very different. But it has also been pointed out that had Louis decided against fleeing at all, this too could have changed the situation considerably. It was the unsuccessful flight which triggered the chain of events leading inevitably to his death. Nostradamus seems to have seen this quite clearly. Century 8, quatrain 87 reads:

> The fatal conspiracy will come to full effect
> Responsibility given and the journey of death
> Elected, created and received by his followers, he will then be defeated
> The blood of the innocent is before the eyes in remorse

The verse is almost self-explanatory. Louis was elected and in that sense created by his subjects, who then proceeded to defeat him following a journey that set the seal on his death. But Louis was little more than a pawn of history, a monarch who may have been weak, but was essentially innocent of much wrong-doing.

In quatrain after quatrain, Nostradamus remorselessly

chronicles the events that followed the 'fatal flight'. Quatrain 19 of Century 8 tells how the royal family was almost completely wiped out and those 'redder than red' (i.e. the followers of Robespierre) annihilated the more moderate revolutionaries. Quatrain 59 of Century 3 tells of a government turned barbarous after it had been usurped by the Third Estate (the Commons) and put to death numerous victims, most of its own kind.

And then, in quatrain 57 of Century 1, comes the death of the King.

Great discord shakes the land —
The agreement broken, lifting his face to heaven
The bleeding mouth swims with blood
The face anointed with milk and honey lies on the ground

This is a verse unmatched for its horror. At a time of great discord, the constitutional agreement between Louis and the National Assembly was broken. The King climbed the scaffold and lifted his face to heaven while reciting the third verse of the third Psalm, 'But thou, O Lord, art a shield for me; my glory, and the lifter up of mine head'.

As the guillotine fell, blood fountained from Louis' mouth. Then the head, anointed with milk and honey on the day of his coronation, lay severed on the ground. The Prophet then goes on to describe, in quatrain 92 of Century 6, how the King's head was buried in quicklime, as happened in actuality in the cemetery of the Madeleine, centuries after the grisly prediction was made.

# 9
# First Antichrist

There is an apocalyptic aspect to the prophecies of Nostradamus. Many books and articles claim – albeit inaccurately, as we shall see – that he foresaw the end of the world in 1999, a prophecy which has religious and millennial linkages. We shall return to the end of the world presently, but for the moment it is worth noting that the Catholicism of Nostradamus did indeed have an apocalyptic tinge. He accepted, as did almost all his contemporaries, there would be a literal Second Coming of Christ. Dr David Pitt Francis[25] has argued that a number of his predictions are based on biblical prophecies of Armageddon and the Antichrist. But if so, he gave them a peculiarly personal twist. He believed there would not be one Antichrist, but three.

Most commentators consider the first of them was Napoleon Bonaparte.

Napoleon was born on August 15, 1769, to Carlo and Letizia Buonaparte at Ajaccio in Corsica. After a year at the Military Academy in Paris, he was commissioned second lieutenant in artillery in 1785.

During the heady, dangerous days of the French Revolution which Nostradamus foresaw so clearly, Bonaparte had strong revolutionary sympathies and in September 1793 assumed command of an artillery brigade at the siege of Toulon. Within three months, the British were driven out and Napoleon was promoted to General of Brigade. In February, 1794, he was assigned to the French army in Italy.

On October 5, 1795, a revolt broke out in Paris. Napoleon efficiently routed the insurrectionists within four months and was rewarded with the post of Commander of the Army of the Interior. It was around this time that he married the 33-year-old widow, Josephine de Beauharnais.

In the early spring of 1796, Bonaparte defeated the Sardinians at Mondovi. Then, in a demonstration of extraordinary military brilliance, he won Lombardy from the Austrians. As he crossed the Alps to advance on Vienna, the Austrians panicked and sued successfully for an armistice. Bonaparte personally negotiated the Treaty of Campo Formio in October, 1797.

But Napoleon did not confine himself to military matters. He created the Cisalpine Republic in northern Italy and negotiated treaties with various rulers. He also looted money and Italian works of art to enhance French museums and to bolster French finances.

On his return to Paris, the Directory proposed an invasion of England, but Napoleon urged the occupation of Egypt instead. He reached Egypt at the beginning of July 1, occupied Alexandria and Cairo, guaranteed Islamic law, and began to reorganize the government. But exactly one month later, Britain's great Admiral Horatio Nelson attacked and annihilated the French fleet at Abukir Bay. Bonaparte calmly continued his administrative reorganization.

In February 1799, Bonaparte invaded Syria to forestall a Turkish attack on Egypt, but was halted at Acre by Turkish troops under British command. A plague-ridden French army returned to Cairo in June. With news of increasing problems at home, Napoleon sailed for France on August 24.

On his arrival, he joined in a conspiracy to overthrow the Directory. Just under a month later, he was appointed Commander of the Paris garrison and the five Directory members resigned. The following day Bonaparte used troops to disperse the assemblies and accepted appointment as one of three Consuls.

Although the Consulate guaranteed law and order, Bonaparte concentrated power in his own hands. He centralized local government, pacified the rebellious regions, reconciled the royalists and participated in drawing up the Napoleonic Code, a complete codification of the civil law.

In June 1800, he defeated the Austrians at Marengo and within two years had concluded beneficial peace treaties with both Austria and Britain. A grateful populace made him Consul for Life on August 2, 1802.

It was not enough for a growing ego. Bonaparte set about extending French influence into Holland, Switzerland, and Savoy-Piedmont, which he actually annexed. He extended his country's colonial empire, mainly by recovering Haiti. A disgruntled Britain went to war again in 1803.

Bonaparte organized a 170,000-strong army to invade Britain, but failed to draw the British fleets away from their home base. When Austria prepared to resume war, he was forced to abandon his invasion plans. His fortunes plunged further when Admiral Nelson won the Battle of Trafalgar in 1805.

Following an unsuccessful assassination attempt, the Senate asked Bonaparte to establish a hereditary dynasty. On December 2, 1804, he crowned himself emperor and created a titled court that included many of his statesmen and generals as well as ex-royalists. Over the next few years he placed members of his family on the thrones of Naples, Holland, Westphalia, and Spain and married his relatives to some of the most distinguished families in Europe. Having divorced Josephine in 1809, he married Marie Louise, daughter of Austrian Emperor Francis I.

Encouraged by Nelson's victory, Britain organized a Third Coalition against France, but Napoleon's new Grand Army destroyed both the Austrian and Russian armies in the fighting which ensued. Venice and Dalmatia were annexed to Napoleon's Kingdom of Italy, and in 1806, he created the Confederation of the Rhine, a grouping of German states under French protection. A thoroughly worried Prussia organized a

Fourth Coalition against Napoleon late in 1806, but its forces were destroyed in the Battle of Jena-Auerstadt. After going on to defeat the Russians, Napoleon forced the allies to sign the Treaties of Tilsit, which resulted in the creation of the Grand Duchy of Warsaw and the Kingdom of Westphalia.

Napoleon was now dominant in Europe, but Britain remained a thorn in his flesh. In 1806, he instituted a blockade of British trade. Portugal refused to observe it, France intervened in Iberia and became embroiled in the Peninsular War. Austria mobilized and began the War of the Fifth Coalition. Although most historians agree Napoleon's overall political strategy was flawed at this period, the final outcome was nevertheless a French victory.

But Russia had also refused to join in the trade sanctions against Britain and Napoleon invaded Russia in June of 1812. The Russian armies withdrew, drawing Napoleon deeper and deeper into the wastelands of their immense country. Napoleon reached Moscow, but waited in vain for Emperor Alexander I to surrender. Russian arsonists set the wooden city on fire. Napoleon ordered a retreat in October. He escaped Russian encirclement, but the savage Russian winter decimated his army. There was more bad news awaiting him. The demented General Claude Malet mounted an abortive coup in Paris, then the Prussians denounced their alliance with the French. Before long he was facing a Sixth Coalition of Prussia, Russia, Britain, and Sweden. Incredibly, Napoleon raised a new army and defeated the allies at Lutzen and Bautzen, but was eventually defeated in the Battle of Nations. In 1814, France was invaded. Although Napoleon again defeated each enemy army as it advanced on Paris, he was hopelessly outnumbered. The allies took Paris on March 31. Napoleon abdicated and was exiled to the island of Elba.

He decided to return to France in 1815. King Louis XVIII fled and Napoleon occupied Paris on March 20. The allies immediately prepared for war. At first all went well for Napoleon, then the Duke of Wellington stepped in and roundly defeated the French at the Battle of Waterloo.

Napoleon returned to Paris, where he abdicated for the second time on June 23. He was exiled to the island of Saint Helena and died there on May 5, 1821.

One's views of a great military leader tend to depend on whether or not he is fighting on your side. There were powerful figures in Victorian Britain who believed literally that he was the Antichrist predicted in the Book of Revelation. The French were – and still are – understandably less sure. Although his ambition cost hundreds of thousands of French lives, he nevertheless established many institutions which survive to the present day and probably did more for French prestige than any other leader in history. Why then should Nostradamus, patriot to the core, consider him an Antichrist as well?

The plain fact is that Nostradamus was a royalist first and a patriot second. He considered Napoleon, like all the French revolutionaries, a usurper. Thus all his military genius was summed up by the prophet in one word . . . butcher.

> An Emperor will be born near Italy
> Who will cost his Empire dear
> Having seen those who support him, they will say
> He is less of a prince than a butcher

Century 1, Quatrain 60

As we have already seen, this French Emperor was certainly 'born near Italy' in Corsica. Those who supported him in his first steps to power were the French revolutionaries of whom Nostradamus profoundly disapproved. But was he really writing of Napoleon – there have, after all, been many emperors who deserved the adjective 'butcher'? In the first quatrain of Century 8, Nostradamus leaves us no room for doubt by naming Napoleon in an anagram:

> Pau, Nay, Loron more fire than blood will be
> In praise to swim, the great man will flee to the confluence.

He will refuse entry to the pies
And the depraved ones of France will keep them confined

As Erika Cheetham points out, Pau, Nay and Loron are all towns in western France, but the verse makes no sense at all if interpreted this way. When Nostradamus' known love of anagrams is taken into consideration, however, Pau, Nay, Loron becomes 'Napaulon Roy'. The spelling 'Napaulon' is Corsican and was by no means uncommon. Thus the phrase translates 'Napoleon the King'.

Given this interpretation, the verse is a rich vein of meaning. John Hogue makes the interesting suggestion that the reference to fire and blood in the first line points both to Nostradamus' astrological and to his royalist interests – as a Leo, Napoleon was born under a fire sign, but was not of 'the blood', i.e. the blood royal with which the prophet himself was so obsessively concerned.

The word 'pies' in line 3 is a colloquial French diminutive of 'magpies' which, in the original, shares the same spelling as the name Pius. This links the verse immediately with two Popes, Pius VI and VII, both of whom were actually imprisoned by Napoleon in his capacity as head of what Nostradamus would certainly have considered a depraved state. There is even an explanation of the curious term 'confluence' in that Pius VI was taken to Valence to die on the confluence of the rivers Rhône and Isère.

As we saw in the last chapter, Nostradamus displayed an ability to focus on the human dimension of great events as well as their broader outlines. His prevision of the flight to Varennes was packed with greater detail than any other prophecy of the Revolution. In that case, the precognition was influenced by Nostradamus' known respect for and interest in the French royal family. When we come to examine his predictions about the Napoleonic era, essentially the same quirk emerges; but here, since the royal family had given way to a usurper, the focus of interest was the fate of Popes.

Roman Pontiff, beware of approaching
A city which is bathed by two rivers
Your blood will be brought up
You and yours when blooms the rose

Century 2, Quatrain 97

This could hardly be clearer. The Roman Pontiff, Pope Pius VI, was taken with thirty-two priests to Valence which is bathed, as we have just noted, by the Rhône and the Isère. There he died, vomiting blood, on August 29, 1799, the summer season when roses bloom.

Nostradamus was quite obviously appalled by the fate of God's Vicar on Earth at the hands of Napoleon, for he returns to the circumstances again. In one of the most difficult, but at the same time most remarkable, of all his verses, he wrote:

Montgolfier will go forth against the one from the Aventine
With one beneath the hole who will act as a military observer
Between two rocks will spoils of war be taken
From the sixth celibate whose power is in decline

Century 5, Quatrain 57

While I have taken some liberties in the translation of this verse, which is unusually badly structured even for Nostradamus, there is no denying the essential content – and this content is almost chilling in its precision. The world's first hot air balloon was invented by the French Montgolfier brothers in 1783. Eleven years later, the invention was put to military use during the Battle of Fleurus when a military observer was suspended beneath the hole at the bottom of the balloon to spy on the opposing army.

The 'sixth celibate' was Pius VI, the first Pope to bear that number since Nostradamus composed his quatrains. He was 'the one from the Aventine' (i.e. Rome) against whom the Montgolfier balloon ultimately went forth since the battle proved the turning point in the first phase of the Revolutionary Wars and led indirectly to the Pope being deprived of the twin rocks of his power; Avignon and his Italian holdings. These circumstances were themselves spelled out directly by Nostradamus in another of his quatrains:

Around the great city
There will be soldiers in the fields and in the towns
To give assault is Paris incited against Rome
And the Pontificate will be greatly pillaged

Century 5, Quatrain 30

The prediction came true with a vengeance. When rioters killed the French General Duphot, his colleague General Berthier moved on Rome, which was already encircled by his troops. The Vatican was pillaged, the Pope dispossessed and imprisoned. These were extraordinarily difficult times for the Catholic Church. When Pius VI died at Valence, the College of Cardinals had been more or less broken up by the Revolution. All the same, a Conclave was proclaimed in Venice and a new Pope, Pius VII, elected. History records that he too was to fall foul of Napoleon, by then First Consul of France. Once again, Nostradamus had specifically predicted the events centuries before. There were two relevant quatrains in his published *Centuries* when French troops moved into Rome for the second time:

Par l'univers sera fait un monarque
Qu'en paix et vie ne sera longuement
Lors se prendra la piscature barque
Sera regie au plus grand detriment

Century 1, Quatrain 4

En naviguant captif prins grand Pontife
Grand après faillir les clercs tumultuez
Second esleu absent son bien debiffe
Son favory bastard à mort tué

Century 5, Quatrain 15

Both James Laver and Erika Cheetham interpret the opening line of the first of these quatrains as referring to Napoleon himself. Laver translates it as 'A universal monarch will be set up', while Cheetham renders it as 'In the world there will be made a king'. I am not entirely happy with either version. The literal translation is 'By the universe there will be made a monarch' which is close to both, but still holds the possibility of a different interpretation.

Laver's 'universal monarch', which is an appealing construction, is taken to refer to Napoleon as Emperor, since he went on to conquer so much of Europe. But it might be argued that Nostradamus, with his respect for the Papacy, would more readily apply the term to the Pope, whom he would rate more highly than any secular king, however powerful. Against this background, I would suggest a more accurate interpretation of the verse would be:

> By the Pope there will be made a king
> Who will not long enjoy peace or even life
> Then will be taken the Fisherman's Boat
> Which will be managed to its great detriment

The second of the two quatrains is less troublesome. It translates along the lines:

> While travelling, the great Pope will be made captive
> His clergy will fall into confusion
> He, the second elected one absent, will suffer a decline of fortune
> By his favourite bastard to death put

The facts of the situation were that while Napoleon crowned himself King/Emperor of France on May 18, 1804, he insisted that Pope Pius VII attend the ceremony to legitimize his claim. Whether the second line of the first verse refers to Emperor or Pope is unimportant – neither was destined to enjoy a peaceful life. The 'Fisherman's Boat' was the Boat of Peter, a poetic reference to the Papacy itself, which was certainly mismanaged by the unfortunate Pius VII.

The second verse is even more specific. Pius VII, one of two Popes to travel to France, was made captive in 1808, an act which caused his clergy to be thrown into a tumult. Pius was the second elected Pope to be absent from Rome when his fortunes declined – his predecessor, Pius VI, was also imprisoned by Napoleon. The phrase 'favourite bastard' would reflect Nostradamus' displeasure at the Pope's involvement in the coronation of an upstart with no legitimate claim to the throne and must therefore refer to Napoleon himself. If so, it is plainly inaccurate since Pius VII was not put to death by Napoleon and eventually gained his release from prison on the Emperor's abdication in 1814. Laver explains the line rather feebly by suggesting the Pope was only put to death metaphorically in that he lost his political influence. My own feeling is that, peering through the distorting mists of time, Nostradamus simply confused two Popes: it was Pius VI, not VII, who died miserably in Napoleon's jail.

I have devoted considerable attention to these Papal predictions since they are further illustrations of the way in which the prophet's talents manifested. His personal interest in such matters as the fate of kings and Popes turned his attention to specific details within the great panoramas he surveyed. But this certainly does not mean he missed the wood for the trees. Scattered throughout the *Centuries* is a broad delineation of Napoleon's rise and fall.

> Quite a different type of man will attain to the Great Empire
> Unkind, unhappy
> Ruled by one come only a short time to his bed
> While the kingdom rushes to disaster

Century 6, Quatrain 67

Napoleon was, as Nostradamus foresaw, a very different type

of monarch for France, since he had no claims to royal blood. The picture of his personality that has come down to us through contemporary accounts is of a brooding, lonely, unhappy man, sometimes strongly influenced by the women who came to his bed (notably Josephine). While his military talents certainly enabled him to extend the Empire, the end result was misfortune.

> Bearing a name which no French King passed on to him
> More fearsome than a thunderbolt
> Terrorizing Italy, Spain and England
> Of a foreign woman greatly attentive
>
> Century 4, Quatrain 54

It is, of course, common practice for monarchs to take the same names as illustrious predecessors. Thus we find France ruled by a succession of kings by the name of Louis, differentiated by number, in the same way that one discovers more than one Charles or Edward in the list of British kings. But Bonaparte was the first French king to bear the name Napoleon . . . a name no other King has passed on to him. As a military strategist, he was indeed to prove more fearsome than a thunderbolt, terrorizing Italy, Spain and Britain among others. The mention of a 'foreign woman' probably refers to the Austrian Marie Louise.

> From the marine city held in tribute
> The shaven-headed man will take his power
> To put to flight the sordid one who will then oppose him
> For fourteen years he will maintain his tyranny
>
> Century 7, Quatrain 13

The marine city held in tribute was Toulon, which Napoleon recaptured from the English in December, 1793. The shaven-headed man was Napoleon himself who, Nostradamus noted, wore his hair cropped far shorter than the traditional style for

French Emperors. Oddly enough, it was his military success at Toulon which formed the initial foundation for his reputation and, in that sense, he drew all his subsequent power from Toulon. He seized power in the coup d'état of November 1799 and held it until his abdication in April 1814 – his fourteenth year.

These quatrains are general predictions of Napoleon's career, but Nostradamus penned several more that dealt with specifics.

> The great Po shall be greatly troubled by a French warrior
> Futile terror to the seafaring Lion
> Great numbers of men will travel by sea
> But a quarter of a million of them will never come back

Century 2, Quatrain 94

The River Po is in northern Italy where, as we have seen, Napoleon scored many of his earliest military successes. He then decided to attack British interests in Egypt and great numbers of his men travelled by sea to that country, causing considerable consternation to Britain (the 'seafaring Lion') whose navy attempted unsuccessfully to stop him. It is difficult to say with certainty how many of Napoleon's men were lost in his campaigns at this period, but reliable estimates suggest the figure must have been at least half a million.

When the French expeditionary force sailed, it launched an opportunist, but highly successful attack on Malta, then held by the Knights of Rhodes. Nostradamus foresaw it clearly:

> Saturn and Mars will be in Leo and Spain held captive
> Taken in war by a leader in Libya
> Close to the time when in Malta, those of Rhodes are taken alive
> And Roman rule will be smashed by the Cock

Century 5, Quatrain 14

The opening line is a typical enough astrological calculation, but the period of the prediction is more easily determined by the fact that Spain was occupied during the Peninsular War of 1807/1808. Although the 'leader in Libya' is obscure unless Nostradamus confused his Middle Eastern countries while studying visions of Napoleon in Egypt, the rest is straightforward enough, and accurate. The Knights of Rhodes were taken alive on Malta, while the Treaty of Tolentino signalled the break-up of Vatican secular power at the insistence of France, a country whose emblem is the Cock.

In a curious attempt to warn his country against blindly following Napoleon, Nostradamus penned this verse:

If, France, you pass beyond the Ligurian sea
You will find yourself surrounded both on islands and at sea
Those of Islam will face you, and more importantly, Adriatic attack
So you will be forced to chew the bones of asses and horses

*Century 3, Quatrain 23*

Napoleon, who certainly believed in oracles, nonetheless ignored the advice and was faced with attack by the Islamic Turks and the British fleet which sailed from its former position in the Adriatic. His men were besieged on the island of Malta and again at Alexandria where hunger was one of the greatest difficulties they faced. Perhaps Nostradamus was thinking of this time when he lectured France in Quatrain 24 of Century 3, never to attempt such an expansion again:

From this enterprise great confusion
Great loss of people and treasure
You must never again extend there
France, make memorable what I say to you

The nature of the disaster which befell the French forces at this time is indicated in another, highly explicit quatrain:

The leader who brought a large army
Far from the skies of home to a place of strange customs and language
Will have only five thousand left in Crete and Thessaly
The leader will save himself by flight on a wooden ship

Century 1, Quatrain 98

The curious fact is that by June 1799, Napoleon's huge expeditionary army to Egypt had been reduced to about five thousand men by the action of the Turks who were then masters of Crete and Thessaly. To claim that Napoleon saved himself by fleeing on a wooden ship is perhaps a little unfair, even given that Nostradamus disliked him so much, but the fact remains that he did set sail for home in August of that year, leaving many immediate problems behind.

By the time he came to write quatrain 77 of Century 1, Nostradamus was recording his vision of the Battle of Trafalgar. His clairaudience failed to pick up the name, but he seems to have seen the site clearly enough.

Between two seas lies a promontory of land
A man dies by the bridle of a horse
Lord Neptune unfurls a black sail
While the fleet lies between Gibraltar and Cape Roche

Trafalgar is a promontory between two seas and the Battle of Trafalgar was fought between Gibraltar and Cape Roche. 'Neptune' may have been 'Nelson' misheard, but even if not, there is a certain poetic appeal in the thought of the god of the sea unfurling a black sail to mark the death of the great Admiral. It is also possible that Nostradamus may have been referring literally to the British flagship which actually unfurled a black sail at the time.

The most curious detail of all is contained in the second line. Some historians insist that Admiral Villeneuve, who commanded the French fleet, was strangled by one of Nelson's Mamelukes at an inn in Rennes in 1806. Whether or not this actually occurred, it is certainly true to say that when a Mameluke sought revenge, he traditionally sought to strangle his enemy using the bridle of a horse.

Trafalgar marked a distinct downturn in Napoleon's fortunes as Nostradamus faithfully recorded in quatrain 1 of Century 3 where he states that the great maritime power would reach a pinnacle following the naval battle, while her revolutionary adversary would grow pale with fear.

Military historians have often remarked that Napoleon's really critical mistake was his invasion of Russia. He was lured too deeply into that vast wasteland, and the bleak Russian winter eventually decimated his army in a way that the combined forces of multiple European coalitions had never achieved. As always, it seems, Nostradamus saw it coming:

> The part of Rome ruled by he who interprets the Augur
> By the French will be much troubled
> But the French nation will rue the hour
> Of the North Wind and the fleet when they drive too far

Century 2, Quatrain 99

'He who interprets the Augur' is the successor to the Pontifex Maximus of Ancient Rome, i.e. the Pope. The part of Rome over which he rules is the Vatican, which was indeed sorely troubled by the French under Napoleon, as we have already seen. But Nostradamus correctly foresaw that if the French pushed too far, they were in danger both from the chill north wind of the Russian winter and the nautical skills of the British fleet.

Napoleon did indeed push too far and although he laid waste to Moscow (aided by the scorched earth policy of Russian arsonists) a flame of freedom had been ignited by the courage of the Russian people. Napoleon's reputation for invincibility had burst like a bubble. As the remnants of his Grande Armée staggered back across the border, it was obvious that their

General's dream of conquest, so reminiscent of expansionist Rome under the Caesars, was now in shreds. And as the troops returned there was, it seems, an invisible observer. Nostradamus wrote:

A mass of men approach from Slavonia
The Destroyer has ruined the ancient city
His Roman dream rendered desolate
He will not know how to extinguish this great flame

Century 4, Quatrain 82

It would be tortuous to quote every quatrain which relates to Napoleon: Nostradamus treated the detail of his life like an enthusiastic biographer. He foresaw the Sixth Coalition of Russia, Prussia, Britain and Sweden following Napoleon's retreat from Moscow; he seems to have watched Wellington fight his way through Spain; and he predicted the British capture of Aquitaine in a punning quatrain in which he renamed the province 'Anglaquitaine'. He foresaw details like Napoleon's betrayal by his brother-in-law, Murat, King of Naples.

And as if that were not enough, he spelled out the Emperor's exile to Elba, his return from that small island, his famous Hundred Days of renewed rule and his second – and final – exile to Saint Helena where, as Nostradamus put it, he finally laid down his sceptre. Quatrain piles upon quatrain to form an impressive record of the most destructive human being of his age, a man whose driving ambition, ruthlessness and arrogance justly earned him the epithet Antichrist. But Nostradamus' visions did not end with the first Antichrist. He insisted that, however dreadful Napoleon may have been, there were substantially more evil men to come.

# 10

# Changing Times

A picture is beginning to emerge. It is a picture seen from the viewpoint of a dark-eyed, bearded, chauvinistic royalist, Jewish by birth, Roman Catholic by persuasion, born and raised in an era when the sun circled the earth and civilization's most sophisticated technical achievement was the crossbow.

This man was educated in disciplines we would now largely dismiss as superstition, and he accepted, as literal truth, religious doctrines which most modern scholars consider allegorical. His vision of the future comes to us filtered through a mind that, while brilliant, was hide-bound by prejudice and preconception.

At first he examined those things most familiar and closest to his heart: the fate of his King, the destinies of royal children. Next, he concerned himself with what might become of his country; and while he hated his visions, he still retained the intellectual honesty to report back clearly the horrors he foresaw.

He took a sidelong glance at other nations, notably those likely to influence France. Thus he predicted the rise and fall of her near-neighbour, Britain, as an imperial power and chronicled the involvements of countries like Spain and Austria in Gallic affairs. But France remained the centre of his universe and what he saw was always bent to fit his personal philosophy. When the rightful King of France was replaced by a shaven-headed upstart who devastated most of Europe, Nostradamus could not believe anything other than that he was witnessing the brutalities of the Antichrist.

The prophet had no difficulty understanding his initial visions. As a citizen of medieval France, he had experience of pestilence, war, sudden death and the murderous machinations of politics. Up to and including the time of Napoleon, the world must have looked more or less familiar to him. If a soldier's rifle was far more efficient than a sixteenth-century arquebus, it was at least still recognisable as a firearm. Fashions might change, but women still wore cotton, silk and wool. Carriages may have grown less ornate, but they were still pulled by horses.

But by the time the Victorian era was drawing to a close, there were changes occurring destined to transform the world into a place as alien to Nostradamus as the far face of the moon. Watt improved the steam engine. Stephenson built his famous Rocket. Within fifty years, there was a spider's web of railways not alone across the face of Britain, but across most other advanced countries as well.

In an era of rapid change, the supremacy of the railways did not go unchallenged for long. Automotive production on a commercial scale began in France about 1890.

In 1903 the Ford Motor Company was founded in America and Henry Ford's first car, the Model N, was marketed three years later. In 1908 he revolutionized the industry by introducing mass production. Between 1908 and 1927, more than 15 million Model Ts were sold.

What was happening on the roads would have been bewildering to a Nostradamus who took eight weeks to journey from Salon to Paris. But what was happening on the roads was nothing when compared to what was about to happen in the air. He would, of course, have been familiar with the concept of human flight. As an educated man, he must have known the classical myths of Daedalus and Icarus. He may even have heard of the monk Eilmer of Malmesbury who succeeded in making a short gliding flight from Malmesbury Abbey in Wiltshire, sometime around AD 1000. But nothing in his background, philosophy or experience could possibly have prepared him for the outcome of the famous experiment at Kittyhawk in 1903 when the first powered, controllable aircraft was flown by the pioneering brothers, Orville and Wilbur Wright. Within a few short decades, humanity had taken to the air in a big way.

And the revolution in transportation was not the only change the world was undergoing at this time. A technological explosion produced a series of inventions and discoveries in the mid-nineteenth century, including the telegraph, the telephone, and the incandescent lamp. These were built on a type of power that would have been considered magical in Nostradamus' day – electricity.

Changes brought about by technology were reflected by changes in morals, mores, political thought and the fundamental structure of society. Old class distinctions became increasingly less meaningful. There were movements towards centralisation. In country after country, political leaders seized on the new technology, particularly in the realm of communications, to restrict and organise whole populations. Even the old religious certainties, unquestioned by generations of the faithful, were breaking down under the impact of Darwin's evolutionary theories.

And bewildering though it must have seemed to him, Nostradamus foresaw it all. In Quatrain 10 of Century 2, he wrote the following chilling description of modern times:

> Before long everything will be organised
> We await a sinister century
> When the state of the clergy will be changed
> And few will be found who want to stay in their places

Nor had he lost his eye for detail, although he was now peering through time across a gulf of almost four centuries. He was even able to pick up an important name.

The lost thing is found, having been concealed for centuries
Pasteur will be honoured like a demi-god
This will come about when the moon is at the end of the
Great Cycle
But rumours will then dishonour him

Century 1, Quatrain 25

The French chemist Louis Pasteur was the founder of microbiology. His development of germ theory was one of the most significant steps in modern medicine. In 1854, he became professor of chemistry and nine years later Dean of the Lille Faculty of Science, where he showed that yeast was a microorganism and not a chemical catalyst, as had been widely believed. In a paper entitled *Memoire Sur la Fermentation Appelée Lactique* published in 1858, he suggested that as each type of fermentation was caused by a particular kind of microorganism, or germ, many diseases were also caused by specific germs. Pasteur went on to show by experimentation that all microorganisms arise from other microorganisms and that spoilage of perishable substances could be averted by destroying the microorganisms and preventing further contamination. This discovery resulted in the development of pasteurization. Pasteur also discovered the organism responsible for anthrax, a deadly disease of cattle and humans, and proved that immunization was possible with a weakened strain of the bacillus. He campaigned for hygiene, sanitation, and sterilization to halt the spread of disease-producing bacteria and in 1882 he showed that rabies was caused by an organism too small to be seen even with a microscope. By 1885 he had made the first use of his vaccine against rabies, thus laying the foundation for a study of viruses. Louis Pasteur was born two days after Christmas in 1822 and died in September 1895. The dates are significant, since they place virtually all his working life within the astrological Great Lunar Cycle, which ended in 1889. So the dating is accurate and the name correct: how then does Nostradamus fare on the remainder of his prophecy?

As the man who, more than any other, revolutionized the practice of medicine, Pasteur was in his day honoured as a demi-god – Erika Cheetham claims the *Encyclopaedia Britannica* actually uses the phrase in an article about him. But the methods he advocated – notably vaccination – aroused strong feelings among some members of the medical establishment, who certainly sought to discredit him, often by back room whispering campaigns.

Which leaves us with only that curious first line to explain – the lost thing is found, having been concealed for centuries. What Pasteur found was that disease, in many cases, was caused by microorganisms, life-forms, inimical to humanity, too small for the naked eye to see. In his quatrain, Nostradamus is plainly suggesting that such a thing had been known before Pasteur's day, but forgotten for centuries by medical practitioners. Could this be possible?

It must be remembered that Nostradamus was himself a physician, widely read in ancient texts and fascinated by the medical traditions of other countries. Perhaps he had come across one of the basic principles of traditional Tibetan medicine, lost to the West for centuries because of the isolation of that remote land. This principle states that many diseases are caused by an attack of demons so tiny as to be invisible to the naked eye; and that these 'demons' are to be found typically residing in rotting meat . . .

Nostradamus did not fail to note several inventions of this developing new age, including air travel. In Century 2, Quatrain 29 – a verse to which we shall have reason to return later – there appear the words:

 He shall cross through the sky . . .

Other verses, as we shall see presently, predicted aerial warfare.
    Electricity must have baffled him completely, since it was a scientific development for which he had no philosophical foundation. All the same, he made an excellent stab at

explaining his prevision of the new power in Quatrain 44 of Century 3 where he wrote:

The lightning, so harmful in the rod,
From the earth will be taken and held in the air

Lightning is, of course, a violent natural discharge of electrical energy, harmful when it strikes human beings, livestock or property. Interestingly, Nostradamus associates it with the lightning rod or lightning conductor which conventional wisdom insists was not invented until two full centuries after he wrote his predictions.[26] The second line requires a little more analysis since lightning is an aerial phenomenon and cannot, at face value, be extracted from the earth. But Nostradamus was merely trying to make sense of what he saw; and what he saw was coal and oil being taken from the earth to fuel those power stations which produced the lightning energy and sent it out through overhead (i.e. 'in the air') lines.

The advances in science gave a sense of control which generated a substantial air of optimism. There were many among the emerging middle class of Victorian Britain who believed humanity was living in the best of all possible worlds, that the human condition was destined to improve indefinitely and that it was only a matter of time before scientists learned all there was to know about the nature of the universe. But the utopian vision was shattered in the opening years of the twentieth century by the outbreak of the most widespread, vicious and destructive conflict the world had ever known.

The assassination of the Austrian archduke Franz Ferdinand in Sarajevo in 1914 proved to be the spark that ignited World War I. The Great War, as it was called, quickly came to involve all the major powers of Europe and eventually most countries of the globe. It was a political blood sacrifice which eventually cost more than 8 million lives and an event which Nostradamus could scarcely have missed as he discussed the future with the god who visited the attic room in Salon. Nor, it seems, did he.

The first hint of his insights comes in two obscure lines of Quatrain 54, Century 1:

> The moving Sign enters its House
> Equally favouring both sides

The 'moving Sign' referred to is the astrological Sign of Libra, the Scales, which governs, among other things, the country of Austria. Cheetham argues that Nostradamus was warning that even the influence of balance would not be strong enough to overcome the machinations of the 'evil scythebearer' (the planet Saturn) mentioned earlier in the quatrain. If this seems a little strained, it is as well to know that Nostradamus returns to the theme of Saturn and its influence in Quatrain 80, Century 1 which reads in full:

> From the sixth bright celestial light [i.e. Saturn]
> There will come to Burgundy [i.e. France] stormy times
> At this time a monster will be born of a most hideous beast
> March, April, May, June brings great wounding and trouble

This is somewhat clearer. In astrological doctrine, Saturnine influences tend towards ill fortune, sometimes disaster. Nostradamus foresaw a time of Saturn's rule, which modern astrologers confirm occurred in the second decade of the twentieth century,[27] when France would face great trouble. The precise historical sequence of events which followed the archduke's assassination were these: First, Austria accused the Serbian government of having instigated the assassination and delivered an ultimatum demanding a virtual protectorate over Serbia. Serbia accepted all but one of the demands, but its response was unsatisfactory to Austria-Hungary which declared war. Russia immediately ordered mobilization against Austria, whereupon, Germany declared war on Russia. Russia's ally, France, then began to mobilize, prompting Germany to declare war on France. Stormy times indeed.

This was the time, said Nostradamus, when a monster – the Great War – would be born of a most hideous beast. Historians specializing in the period have frequently wondered at the blindness, arrogance and stupidity of the European powers who ushered the world towards war as carelessly as children playing with matches on a heap of gunpowder. From the turn of the century, crisis followed crisis in an almost unbelievable sequence.

In 1904, the formation of the Anglo-French Entente alarmed Germany, which tried to isolate France by supporting Moroccan independence. Britain rallied to support the French. A second Moroccan crisis erupted in 1911, when a German gunboat entered Agadir seeking compensation for alleged violations of the Algeciras agreement. Britain responded with a strong warning, but the French and Germans negotiated an agreement by which Germany received minor compensation. Another point of tension was the Balkans. During the early 1900s, relations between Serbia and Austria-Hungary deteriorated. A crisis developed in 1908 when Austria-Hungary annexed the former Turkish provinces of Bosnia and Herce-govina. The annexation outraged Serbia and Montenegro, which had regarded the provinces as potential elements of a united Slav state in the Balkans. Russia backed Serbia, and Germany affirmed its support of Austria-Hungary. Military action was avoided, but only just.

In 1912, Serbia, Bulgaria, Greece, and Montenegro formed the Balkan League for protection against Turkey. The first Balkan War erupted shortly after. Fearing a spread of hostilities, the great powers intervened to terminate the war by the Treaty of London in 1913. Within a month a second war began, when Bulgaria opened surprise offensives against Serbia and Greece.

Romania and Turkey joined Greece and Serbia so that Bulgaria was quickly defeated and overrun. These two wars resulted in renewed antagonism between Bulgaria and the other Balkan states, especially Serbia. It also left all the Balkan states generally dissatisfied because of the interference of the great powers in Balkan politics. No wonder Nostradamus referred to the time as a 'hideous beast'.

March, April, May and June – the spring and early summer – of 1914 was a time of fever-pitch tension throughout Europe with, as Nostradamus predicted, much trouble behind the scenes. That trouble became a literal wounding when Archduke Ferdinand, heir to the Austro-Hungarian throne, paid a state visit to the Bosnian town of Sarajevo. As he drove through the streets in their coach, a Serb terrorist stepped forward and shot both him and his wife. It was a 'great wounding' from which the royal couple died. Trouble did indeed follow.

Nostradamus then goes on to chronicle the course of the war. He wrote:

> Towards France there are British incursions
> With the two deadlocked
> Bad weather and frost make for foul terrain
> A mighty attack is made into Turkey

Century 2, Quatrain 1

When war did break out, it quickly turned into a protracted nightmare. Casualties on both sides were enormous. During the first three weeks of fighting, the Allies lost about a quarter of a million men, the Germans somewhat more. By the end of 1914, Allied losses on the Western Front alone had reached a million. Germany at this stage was faring only just a little better. The long-drawn-out bitter stalemate was beginning.

On October 29, 1914, Turkey declared war on the Allies with a surprise bombardment of the Russian Black Sea coast. Britain responded by annexing Turkish Cyprus. On December 17, she declared a protectorate over Egypt – nominally subject to Turkey – and began moving troops in to defend the Suez Canal.

Turkey's alignment with Germany closed the Dardanelles to the Allies, separating Russia from Britain and France. Russia was now almost completely cut off from vitally needed war supplies, while the Allies were anxious to regain access to the Ukrainian grain fields. Winston Churchill, then First Lord of the Admiralty, urged immediate seizure of the Dardanelles. The British War Minister, Lord Kitchener, wanted something done about the stalemated western front and opposed any reduction of strength in the west for what he saw as a peripheral operation in the east. Nevertheless, in early January, the British War Council approved an expedition against the Dardanelles.

It was these circumstances of which Nostradamus wrote in his quatrain. The British were fighting in France. The two opposing sides were deadlocked. The weather was dreadful and a mighty attack was made on the Dardanelles in the hope of breaking through to Constantinople.

This was to be a long, miserable war and Nostradamus seems to have watched it through from the shadows of his study in sixteenth century Provence.

All the army will be exhausted by the long war
So no money will be found for the troops
Instead of gold or silver, leather will be minted
The brass of France and the crescent of the moon

Century 7, Quatrain 25

There is no arguing with the first line: beyond all previous wars, this one proved totally exhausting. 'Sounding brass' is a Biblical phrase which Nostradamus would surely have known, and refers to war. Thus the final line indicates war at once in France and Turkey, where the Muslim troops fought under the crescent flag.

The middle lines are exceptionally interesting. Erika Cheetham suggests they refer to barter on the battlefield while most other commentators simply ignore them. It seems, however, much more likely that Nostradamus was noticing for the first time the widespread use of banknotes and, unable to believe any culture could be so silly as to print them on flimsy paper, decided they must be made of leather.

Circumstances following the ending of the war were seen clearly:

> The horrible war begun in the west
> The year following will come the pestilence
> So dreadful for young, old and beast
> Blood, fire, Mercury, Mars, Jupiter and France

Century 9, Quatrain 55

On August 4, 1914 a specially trained German task force of about 30,000 men crossed the Belgian frontier and attacked Liege, one of the strongest fortresses of Europe. Some of the fortifications were captured in a daring night attack led by Major General Erich Ludendorff. The rest, pounded into submission by giant howitzers, surrendered on August 16. The German First Army under General Alexander von Kluck and the Second, commanded by General Karl von Bulow, poured through the Liège corridor and across the Meuse. Hastily mobilized Belgian field forces were brushed aside, and Brussels was occupied on August 20. Thus began, in the west, the horrible war foreseen by Nostradamus.

It ended in 1918, but before the world could catch its breath, the pestilence forecast by Nostradamus appeared in the form of a viral influenza epidemic which actually killed more people – young and old – than the hostilities of the previous four years. Astrologically speaking, the conjunction of Mercury, Mars and Jupiter boded ill ('blood and fire') for the prophet's beloved France.

But the Great War was not the only momentous political event in the second decade of the twentieth century. Something less spectacular, but arguably more influential, was brewing in Russia – the Communist Revolution of 1917. As always, Nostradamus looked first at the royal family of the day. In quatrain 72 of Century 6 he wrote:

Through the pretence of divine fury
Will the wife of the great one be violated
Judges wishing to damn such a tale
Sacrifice their victim to ignorant prejudice

The 'wife of the great one' was Alexandra Fyodorovna, Empress of Russia, consort of Nicholas II, the last Tsar. She was a determined, narrow-minded reactionary, who dominated her husband. During World War I she became the virtual ruler of Russia, but her interest in the occult brought her under the influence of the sinister monk Grigory Yefimovich Rasputin after he had demonstrated his healing power on her haemophiliac son, the Tsarevich Aleksei. Over a period of time, Alexandra's relationship with Rasputin grew more and more intimate. He was, for example, the only man other than her husband she was prepared to receive in her bedroom unannounced. Despite his monkish habit, Rasputin was no celibate: his dynamic personality had helped him seduce scores of bored society women and he had a habit of drinking and whoring among the Gypsies. Inevitably, rumours began to circulate that he had made the Tsarina his mistress, violating the royal person under the cloak of ministering to her religious needs. This was a theory to which Nostradamus evidently subscribed.

Whatever the truth of the relationship, it was one which disturbed many people, including the revolutionaries who eventually seized power in Russia. And, as we shall see in the next quatrain, they did indeed end any gossip by the brutal expedient of sacrificing its victim.

The blood of innocents, widow and virgin
So much evil committed by the Reds
Holy icons placed over lighted candles
In terror, more will be seen to move

Century 8, Quatrain 80

Faced with a deteriorating situation at home and abroad, Tsar Nicholas II abdicated in March, 1917. On the night of July 16, 1918, he was shot in the cellar of a house in Sverdlovsk on the orders of his country's new masters, the Bolshevik Reds. Minutes later, his widow and their children were also shot. Surviving documents indicate that during the period of their imprisonment, when it became obvious they must soon die, the adolescent daughters of the Tsar and Tsarina bemoaned the fact that they had never known the physical love of a man. They were virgins.

This, to Nostradamus, was the ultimate evil committed by the Bolshevik Revolution which, like the French Revolution before it, outlawed religion and burned its holy icons. And, perhaps with a glance towards the rise of Stalin, the subjugation of Eastern Europe and the Cold War, he predicted more evil was to come.

Not all the evil was, however, political. In Quatrain 28 of Century 8, Nostradamus foresaw financial problems as well:

> The imitations of gold and silver inflate
> And after the crime are thrown in the lake
> It is discovered that all is exhausted by debt
> And all scripts and bonds wiped out

This is a truly remarkable prediction, given the age in which it was made, an age in which paper money itself, let alone the phenomenon of inflation, was quite unknown in Europe. What event did Nostradamus forecast in this quatrain? By far the most likely candidate is the Great Depression of the 1930s, a slump that remains unique in its magnitude and consequences to this day. At its worst, in 1933, unemployment world-wide ranged between 15 per cent and 25 per cent of the total labour force. In America, then the richest nation on earth, national income fell by half between 1929 and 1932 and there were more than 85,000 business failures. There is little agreement among economists on the causes of the depression. Some thought

World War I might be the culprit. Others looked to the boom of the 1920s. Still others thought money simply went through historical cycles of boom and bust. What remained certain were the effects.

As world trade dropped, country after country turned to nationalist economic policies that only increased their difficulties. Nowhere were the problems more acute than in Germany which underwent a period of almost unimaginable inflation. So extreme did this become that factory workers were literally forced to use wheelbarrows to carry home the mountain of near worthless paper that represented a week's pay. As Nostradamus rightly predicted in an era when the only country to use paper money was China, all scripts and bonds were wiped out. In four short lines, the prophet of Salon had done better in his forecasting than the economists who watched it happen.

# 11
# Rise of Fascism

In 1936 Europe was still a tinder-box of conflicting interests and a continent bristling with arms. World War I had not proven, as was widely hoped at the time, the 'war to end all wars'. What had changed was the political dynamic. The old royal dynasties which had ruled for so long were largely swept away or rendered almost powerless. In their place came followers of new creeds – Communism in Russia and Eastern Europe and an even darker doctrine, Fascism, elsewhere.

Fascism first developed in Italy as a reaction against the spread of Communism and the changes brought about by World War I. Its name was derived from the fasces, an ancient Roman symbol of authority consisting of a bundle of rods and an axe. Nostradamus watched it develop. In Naples, Sicily, Palermo and Syracuse there are new tyrants, he wrote in Quatrain 16 of his second Century. Chief among them was Fascism's Italian founder, Benito Mussolini.

Mussolini was the son of an anticlerical blacksmith with left wing principles. He shared his father's basic views, but expanded them with ideas drawn from philosophers like Nietzsche. In 1912, Mussolini became editor of the Milan Socialist party newspaper *Avanti*. When World War I began, he opposed Italy's involvement at first but then reversed his position and called for entry on the side of the Allies. The stance was not popular with his colleagues who promptly expelled him from the Socialist Party. Mussolini responded by founding his own newspaper, *Il popolo d'Italia*, (which later became the organ of the Fascist movement) and joining the Army. He served until he was wounded in 1917.

In 1919, Mussolini and other war veterans founded a revolutionary, nationalistic group called the Fasci di Combattimento. This new Fascist movement gained support from many landowners, industrialists and army officers. Fascist blackshirt squads carried on local vendettas against Socialists, Communists, Catholics and Liberals. In 1922, they marched on Rome.

On October 28, Mussolini secured a mandate from King Victor Emmanuel III to form a coalition government. During 1925-6, he imposed a single-party, totalitarian dictatorship and awarded himself the title of Il Duce, the Leader. By the mid-1930s, Mussolini had instituted an aggressive foreign policy which led, among other things, to the conquest of Ethiopia and a military alliance with Germany. Although he occupied Albania in April 1939, he kept Italy out of World War II until the middle of 1940, when the Germans seemed certain of winning.

But his judgement was faulty and following a series of Italian military disasters in Greece and North Africa, the leaders of his party abandoned him. He was dismissed from office and arrested on July 25, 1943. Two months later, in a daring raid led by one of their ablest adventurers, the Germans rescued him, and established him as head of a government in northern Italy. But the war was already lost and in April 1945, Mussolini and his mistress, Clara Petacci, tried to flee advancing Allied forces. They were captured by Italian partisans at Lake Como, shot and hanged by their heels in a public square in Milan. Nostradamus followed Il Duce's career with considerable interest and devoted several quatrains to it.

The great one born of Verona and Vincenza
Who carries a most unworthy name
Who at Venice will wish to take vengeance

Is himself taken by the man of the sign

Century 8, Quatrain 33

Verona and Vincenza represent Northern Italy where Mussolini was born. His name literally means 'muslin-maker', a profession considered worthy only of the lower orders in Nostradamus' day. The Axis pact with Germany was sealed near Venice, where it was obvious that Mussolini hoped, with German help, to establish a new Roman Empire and take revenge on those countries he considered to be keeping Italy down. The 'man of the sign' was, of course, the German Fuhrer, who marched beneath the sign of the swastika: it appears that Nostradamus watched the rescue in 1943 which left Mussolini no more than a puppet of his German masters.

Nostradamus was also watching at the beginning of Mussolini's political career. In Century 8, Quatrain 31, he reported:

The first great fruit will be the Prince of Peschiera
But then comes an evil, cruel man
After Venice he will lose his swaggering ways
And will be led into evil by the younger Celin

I have no idea who or what the 'younger Celin' might be, but the Prince of Peschiera is King Victor Emmanuel who held a council of war there in 1917 after the Battle of Caporetto almost brought about Italy's collapse. In a humiliating setback, Italy had lost 40,000 killed and wounded, as well as 275,000 prisoners and probably as many deserters, but the King rejected all defeatist talk, took personal command of his country's forces, and insisted – correctly as it transpired – on fighting to the bitter end.

Unfortunately Victor Emmanuel lived to see his country fall under the influence of the evil, cruel Mussolini. But Mussolini in turn lost influence after he had signed the Axis Pact and was increasingly forced to play second fiddle to German plans.

Nostradamus twice refers to Il Duce by his adopted title. The first of these references comes in Century 6, Quatrain 31:

> The King will discover that which he desires so much
> When the Prelate will be wrongly taken
> Response to the Duce will anger him
> Who in Milan will put several to death

The King, who loathed the strutting Mussolini, took a rather childish delight in angering him, as contemporary documents show. The Prelate wrongly taken was almost certainly Pius XII who maintained a controversial silence during World War II about the extermination of Jews in Nazi Germany. Those put to death in Milan included Count Ciano, the Italian Foreign Minister who was actually married to Mussolini's daughter. Despite his family ties, he joined the conspiracy which unseated Il Duce in July 1943. When Mussolini was reinstated by the Nazis, Ciano was executed.

The second direct reference, in Century 9, Quatrain 95, tells of Mussolini's ultimate fate and is particularly interesting in that Nostradamus got it (at least partly) wrong when he wrote, 'The Duce loses his eyes in an iron cage in Milan'. The line certainly points to Mussolini's violent death, and the picture of someone placed on display – as were the corpses of the Duce and his mistress – is clearly suggested. But the fact remains that Mussolini was shot, then hanged, not placed in a cage. The prophet was, however, quite accurate in placing the death in Milan.

Mussolini was not the only Fascist Nostradamus wrote about and named. Another was Generalissimo Francisco Franco, who led the Nationalist forces in the Spanish Civil War, which broke out in 1936. The Nationalists won and Franco ruled Spain as dictator until his death in 1975. Franco became Spain's youngest general in 1926 at the age of 34, and two years later was named director of the General Military Academy in

Saragossa. He stayed out of the many military conspiracies against the new Spanish Republic until 1936 when, having been appointed Chief of the General Staff by a conservative administration, he was exiled to the Canary Islands by the Popular Front.

When the Nationalist rebellion broke out, Franco flew to Morocco and took over the Spanish garrison. His forces invaded southern Spain and advanced on Madrid. By September Spain was divided between government and Nationalist territories, and the Nationalists established a government of their own. On October 1, they appointed Franco Head of State and Commander in Chief. The war ended in a victory for the Nationalists in 1939.

All this was foreseen by Nostradamus. In Century 9, Quatrain 16, he wrote:

From Castille Franco will drive out the Assembly
The Ambassador will not agree and schism will result
Followers of Rivera will be in the throng
And entry into the great gulf will be prevented

The picture was reinforced in Century 3, Quatrain 54:

One of the greatest will flee to Spain
Which will bleed from a great wound
There will pass troops over the high mountains
All will be laid waste, then in peace he will rule

This is remarkable stuff, even for Nostradamus. When his forces invaded, Franco certainly sought to drive out the existing National Assembly. The greatest of all schisms, civil war, resulted, involving the followers of Primo de Rivera who had become dictator of Spain in 1923. The Spanish Civil War lasted longer and involved more bloodshed than most people had anticipated: it was indeed a great wound which bled profusely. The war was marked by considerable mountain fighting and substantial devastation of the country and its people – when it ended, Franco ordered the execution or imprisonment of hundreds of thousands of Loyalists.

The 'great gulf' mentioned by Nostradamus was possibly a symbolic reference to Communism, of which the prophet could certainly not be expected to approve. Interestingly, when writing of a military man who seized power in such a violent, bloody struggle, Nostradamus insisted Franco would then rule the country in peace. So, somewhat against the odds, it turned out. During World War II Franco kept Spain neutral, although his fascist regime was pro-Axis. In 1955 Spain joined the United Nations and the following year pulled out of northern Morocco. When Franco died on November 20, 1975, his country had enjoyed uninterrupted peace since the ending of the Civil War.

# 12

# Second Antichrist

If Spain was destined for peace in 1939, the same could not be said for the rest of the world. The problem was not so much the spread of Fascism as the development of its particularly vicious and repulsive offshoot, Nazism, the ideology and policies practised by Germany's *Nationalsozialistische Deutsche Arbeiterpartei* (National Socialist German Workers Party) from 1921 to 1945. The aftermath of the First World War produced an atmosphere which left people vulnerable to promises and stimulated the growth of extremist political movements. Among them was the tiny National Socialist German Workers Party, which managed to attract the attention of the Berlin authorities who thought it might be a Communist front.

They sent to investigate an ex-Army corporal who had distinguished himself for his bravery as a messenger in the First World War. He attended two meetings and concluded that, far from a Communist cell, this embryonic Party was an organisation he himself would like to lead. The corporal was Adolf Hitler. Nostradamus, who heard his name chanted down the centuries, may have concluded he was the second Antichrist.

From backroom beginnings in Munich, the National Socialist German Workers Party gathered strength rapidly in the 1930s until it was eventually able to prevent its opponents from forming a majority in the Reichstag, the lower House of

Germany's Parliament. By 1933, the Nazis were in total control.

Nazism comprised nine basic elements:

1 Belief in an Aryan German race superior to all others and destined to rule.
2 Hatred of Jews, who were at once held to be sub-human and responsible for most of Germany's financial ills.
3 Extreme nationalism calling for the unification of all German-speaking peoples.
4 Acceptance of some form of corporate state Socialism.
5 A private army, called the Schutzstaffel, or SS.
6 Emphasis on sports and paramilitary outdoor activities for the young.
7 Massive use of propaganda.
8 Submission of all decisions to a supreme leader.
9 Glorification of strength and discipline.

Although some aspects of Nazism, notably nationalism and anti-Semitism, were already prevalent in Germany, Nazi ideology as a whole was essentially the product of Adolf Hitler himself.

Hitler was born on April 20, 1889, in the Austrian town of Braunau am Inn, the son of a minor customs official. He failed as a student in the classical secondary schools, and again in Vienna in 1907, and was unable to gain admission to the Academy of Fine Arts. In 1913 he went to Munich, where he joined the Bavarian Sixteenth Regiment at the outbreak of World War I. Although Allied propaganda sought to discredit him in later years, he actually distinguished himself for bravery on the western front and was awarded the Iron Cross, First Class. After the war, he joined the National Socialist German Workers Party and quickly became its leader. In 1923 he led the organization into an ill-fated putsch and was imprisoned for his pains. He used his incarceration to write *Mein Kampf*, a political testament in which he defined the enemy as world Jewry, international Communism, effete liberalism, and decadent capitalism. It was a book destined to become the standard text of Nazi philosophy and at the height of Hitler's power actually outsold the Bible in Germany.

Although sentenced to five years, he was released after only nine months. He gathered around himself a devoted core of followers which included the air ace Hermann Goering, the propagandist Joseph Goebbels, the administrator Heinrich Himmler, and the anti-Semitic writer Julius Streicher.

In April 1932, Hitler only narrowly lost the presidential election and elections in July made the Nazis the largest party in the Reichstag. President Hindenburg finally named Hitler Chancellor of Germany on January 30, 1933.

Having won a commanding lead in the last free elections, Hitler dismantled all parties except his own. On June 30, 1934, the infamous 'Night of the Long Knives', he liquidated hundreds of Nazi radicals whom he saw as opposing his will. With the death of Hindenburg in August, he assumed the presidency and adopted the title of Fuhrer, or supreme leader, of the Third Reich.

Hitler's foreign-policy goals were spelled out in *Mein Kampf*: to overturn the Versailles Treaty, unite Germans in a single Greater Germany, destroy Bolshevism, and conquer and colonize eastern Europe. At first he went cautiously, but as the indecisiveness of his opponents became clear, he acted with increasing force. In March 1935 he announced the rearmament of Germany in open violation of the Treaty of Versailles. The following year, without warning, he remilitarized the Rhineland.

In March 1938, he annexed Austria. Later in the year, Britain, France and Italy signed the Sudetenland over to Germany at the Munich Conference. In March 1939, German troops overran the rest of Czechoslovakia. On September 1, Hitler invaded Poland. To his surprise, France and Britain declared war two days later.

At first all went well for the Nazis. Despite a huge standing army, France fell quickly. The Government had placed far too much confidence in the Maginot Line, a series of fortifications built in the late 1920s at a cost of $2,000,000 a mile and based on the (incorrect) premise that should the Germans ever invade, they would do so through Switzerland.

The French authorities might have done better had they read Quatrain 80 of Nostradamus' fourth Century. Here he spelled out clearly how useless the Maginot Line would be:

Near the great river, a great trench, earth excavated
In fifteen different parts the water will be divided
The city taken, fire, blood, cries and battle joined
And the greater part concerned with the clash

The great river was the Rhine, the great trench the Maginot Line. Hitler did not, however, invade through Switzerland, so the whole costly project became irrelevant and the city, Paris, fell when battle was joined, in a welter of fire and blood. By June 1940, Axis control stretched from the Arctic to North Africa, from France to central Europe. For a time it looked as though the Nazis might invade and overrun Britain.

Then the Fuhrer repeated Napoleon's mistake. In June 1941, he cast aside the Nazi-Soviet Pact and invaded the USSR. After early victories, he discovered his army could not fight both the Russian troops and the Russian winter. To make matters worse, by the end of 1941, the United States of America had entered the war.

That was really the beginning of the end for Hitler, although the war still dragged on for years. Finally, in June 1944, the Allies landed on the coast of France. With German defences crumbling in the east and west, Hitler appointed Admiral Karl Doenitz his successor and committed suicide in his underground bunker on April 30, 1945.

The parallels between Napoleon and Hitler are intriguing. Both were born in countries other than those they came to rule. Both had middle class parents. Both were influenced by the political outlook of their fathers, but extended the views to extremes. Both were interested in esoteric subjects and believed in oracles. Both plunged Europe into war. Both achieved substantial victories before they were finally overcome. Both made the fatal error of invading Russia and both were beaten by the Russian winter. In an early quatrain (Century 1, Quatrain 34), the Hitler/Napoleon connection is emphasized when Nostradamus uses the term 'bird of prey', usually reserved for Napoleon, in a verse that almost certainly refers to Hitler:

> The bird of prey flying to the window
> Before conflict with the French makes his preparations
> Some will take him as good, some evil
> The little party will take him as a good omen

The first line is indicative of the situation in the 1930s when Hitler began to show his intentions. For countries less committed to the policy of appeasement, it would have been obvious that a bird of prey was flying at their windows. From his Franco-centred viewpoint, Nostradamus saw Hitler's annexation of Austria, Czechoslovakia and Poland as no more than preparations for his real push into France – which was, in fact, the Fuhrer's first major operation when World War II broke out.

With the wisdom of hindsight, everyone now sees Hitler as the personification of evil, but this was by no means obvious in the 1930s, even outside Germany. As Nostradamus says, some took him to be a good man, others bad.

The final line of the verse is particularly interesting in its choice of phrase. The little (or weak) party was the National Socialist German Workers Party which Hitler joined after World War I. On the night he first attended, total membership was less than twenty and the main topic of discussion was how to raise money since the Party had literally only a few pennies in its coffers. But the National Socialists then, as later, had esoteric as well as political involvements and several of their members entertained a mystical belief in the imminent appearance of a Teutonic messiah who would save the Fatherland and right the wrongs embodied in the Treaty of Versailles. [28] Once Hitler, a spellbinding orator, began to speak at the meetings, these people took it as an omen that the day of the saviour was close and supported his takeover of the Party.

Another quatrain which underlines the similarities between Napoleon and Hitler (in that it could almost apply to either) is Quatrain 35 of Century 3 which reads:

From the depths of Western Europe
To poor people a child will be born
Who with his tongue will seduce a great crowd of people
His reputation towards the Eastern Kingdom will increase

Austria, where Hitler was born, is certainly in the depths of Western Europe; and his parents, like those of Napoleon, were not of the aristocracy. Again like Napoleon, his oratory gained him an enormous following. It is possible that the 'Eastern Kingdom' may be Russia, which was persuaded to conclude a non-aggression treaty with Hitler, but many commentators consider the kingdom in question to be Japan, whose leaders were so impressed by Hitler's reputation that they allied their country to his in the Tripartite Pact.

In Century 3, Quatrain 76, Nostradamus wrote about conditions in Germany under Nazi rule:

In Germany there will arise diverse sects
Which closely approach happy paganism
The heart captive and returns small
They will come back to pay the true title

To certain of the German hierarchy, notably Heinrich Himmler, Nazism was as much a religion as a political creed. At one point in the headlong whirl towards self-destruction, the Reichfuhrer decreed an end to Christian religious practice throughout Germany. He sought to replace the major festivals, notably

Christmas, with a sort of 'happy paganism' devoted to the old Teutonic gods. He advocated placing a swastika on the altar in place of a cross. Himmler would have preferred to abandon any hint of Christian holidays altogether, but felt compelled to hold on to something 'for the sake of the children'.

Although the lunacy of Nazism captured the hearts of the German people for a time, end returns were small in the long term and the country eventually paid an extraordinarily heavy price for its years of madness.

Nostradamus correctly foresaw Hitler's gains and losses:

> He will incorporate into Greater Germany
> Brabant and Flanders, Ghent, Bruges and Boulogne
> After the false truce, the great Russian leader
> Will attack Vienna and Cologne

Century 5, Quatrain 94

This is about as clear as it could be. Hitler's overriding ambition was to create a Greater Germany which stretched across Europe. When World War II broke out, it looked at first as though he might well succeed, for France and Belgium, among several other countries, fell under German domination. The false truce was with Russia: the Fuhrer happily concluded a non-aggression pact which left him free to deal with his enemies in the west, untroubled by the difficulties of a war on two fronts. But when Germany broke the pact and attacked Russia, the eventual result was a push by the Red Army under its 'great leader' Josef Stalin, into Germany itself.

In a similar vein Nostradamus wrote this in Quatrain 90, Century 9:

> A leader of Greater Germany
> Will come to offer false assistance
> A king of kings aiding Hungary
> His war will cause great bloodshed

As leader of Greater Germany, Hitler invaded Poland under the pretext of assisting a supposedly oppressed German minority. He 'helped' Hungary in the same way at a time when the Third Reich had subdued much of Europe and its leader was indeed a 'king of kings'. The final line scarcely needs comment – World War II was the most destructive conflict humanity had ever seen.

There is an intriguing hint that the prophetic doctor may have been privy to Hitler's medical records – or at least listened to rumours which were widespread during the Second World War. In Century 8, Quatrain 15, he wrote:

Towards the North there will be great efforts by the feminine man

To vex almost all of Europe and the world . . .

While there is little doubt that Hitler made great efforts to vex most of Europe and the world, the really interesting element of the verse is the word 'hommasse', translated above as 'feminine man'. In fact, an exact translation is difficult: the word carries shades of meaning beyond the reach of a single English term, or even a short phrase. It suggests a man who is not quite a man, one whose essential virility may be open to question.

There are two areas of comment on this. The first is that historical research suggests Hitler, while aggressively dominant in his political dealings, was a sexual masochist who enjoyed submitting to women to such a degree that he tried to persuade one of his early mistresses to defecate on his face. The other was the widely held belief, incorporated in a popular, if bawdy, British ballad sung to the tune of *Colonel Bogey*,[29] that the Fuhrer had only one testicle and was consequently impotent.

It seems entirely possible that in the attic study of his little medieval house in France, Nostradamus listened to the adoring Nazi crowds who chanted Hitler's name in spectacularly orchestrated rallies. And while the distance in time was too great for him to catch it exactly, he certainly came close. He thought the second Antichrist would be called 'Hister.' In Quatrain 29 of Century 5, he wrote:

Liberty will not be taken back
There will be a black occupation by an iniquitous villain
When the question of the Pontiff is raised
By Hister, Venice will anger the republic

There are several interpretations of this verse – Erika Cheetham believes it deals largely with Hitler's relationship with Mussolini – but I would argue that the real keys are Nostradamus' tendency to see things from the French viewpoint and the likelihood that his visions caused him to telescope future history so events separated by centuries were seen by him as almost side by side.

Given this perspective, it seems that Nostradamus might have been thinking of the French Revolution at the time he wrote of Hitler. For example, the verse following that quoted above (Quatrain 29 of Century 5) deals with an incident during the Revolution. In his mind he would have linked the vicious pursuit of liberty, brotherhood and equality with what, to him, occurred only a visionary eyeblink later. Thus liberty was not achieved as the revolutionaries hoped. Instead there was a 'black occupation', a term which vividly calls to mind the uniforms of the SS Storm Troopers.

The 'question of the Pontiff' refers to the Concordat between Italy (Venice) and the Vatican in 1928. The reference to the question of the Concordat being raised by Hitler is interesting since it is recorded that in the latter stages of the war when he considered attempting to take the whole of Italy, Hitler answered his advisers' objections concerning the Concordat with the remark, 'I will go right into the Vatican!' No wonder Nostradamus thought the Republic – which to him would always have been France – would, as a Catholic country, be angered.

Hitler's name appears in other quatrains, the context of which leave no doubt at all that Nostradamus was viewing the

Nazi period with his prophetic eye.

> Beasts, driven insane with hunger, will cross the rivers
> The greater part of the field will go to Hitler
> In a cage of iron the great will be dragged away
> When the child of Germany observes nothing

Century 2, Quatrain 24

> In a spot not too far removed from Venice
> The two strongest of Asia and Africa
> Will be said to come together with the Rhine and Hitler
> Weeping at Malta and the Ligurian coast

Century 4, Quatrain 68

The first of these verses refers to the war in Europe and its immediate prelude. To take the last two lines first: Hitler was extraordinarily fond of using the term 'iron' in his most impassioned speeches. He spoke of 'iron will', 'iron fist', 'rod of iron' and so on. Nostradamus may have engaged in a little irony on his own account when he spoke of the great (of Europe) being dragged away in a cage of iron – a picturesque account of what did happen in Austria, Czechoslovakia, Poland, etc. when the errant child of Germany decided he would no longer observe national boundaries, treaties, or even the basic rules of international behaviour.

Hitler's blitzkrieg tactics, which consisted of hurling his troops against the enemy in a fierce, smashing blow, were likened to the rush of wild beasts driven mad by hunger. Nostradamus foresaw that, in the early stages of the war at least, the greater part of the field of battle would go to Hitler, who achieved military success after success for the first two years.

The 'spot not too far removed from Venice' in the second quatrain is the Brenner Pass where the Tripartite Axis Pact was signed. The Rhine represents Germany, of course, and the strongest power in Asia at the time was unarguably Japan. The reference to Africa seems strange at first until one remembers that Mussolini's annexation of Ethiopia made Italy the most powerful influence in Africa at the time.

The final line contains war details. The Italians blockaded Malta, which took such a pounding during the war that the entire island was awarded the George Cross for valour. The Ligurian coast came under attack when the Allies bombarded Genoa.

'Every German,' a writer once remarked, 'has one foot in Atlantis.' The comment was certainly true of the Nazi period when interest in the occult ran so high among the political hierarchy that a Pendulum Institute was set up in Berlin to dowse the positions of British and American ships so that they could be intercepted by U-boats. In such an atmosphere, it is scarcely surprising to discover a special relationship with Nostradamus.

The quatrains were studied enthusiastically at two levels. There is no doubt at all they were accepted as genuine prophecies and strenuous attempts were made to determine which of them referred to the events of the 1930s and early 1940s. Ernst Krafft, for example, the Swiss often referred to as 'Hitler's astrologer', telegraphed his Fuhrer with the warning that an assassination attempt would be made on him at a meeting in November, 1939. He drew his basic information from Quatrain 51 of Century 6 which stated:

> People gathered to witness something new
> Princes and Kings among those present
> Pillars and wall cave in, but as by a miracle
> The King is saved and thirty of the onlookers

Krafft's dating of the prophecy was presumably done astrologically since there is nothing in the quatrain itself to give either the month or the year he quoted. But however he did it, he was accurate enough. There actually was an assassination attempt on Hitler in 1939 when he was scheduled to address a public meeting. But the unpredictable Fuhrer cut his visit short so that the bomb exploded well after he left. The verse fits equally well – and arguably even better – the second assassination attempt near the end of the war. Hitler was discussing tactics with top military advisers when a briefcase bomb went off, killing and wounding many, and wrecking the bunker in which they were holding the meeting. At first it was widely reported that the Fuhrer had been killed, but he survived 'as if by a miracle' with no worse damage than a burst eardrum and temporary paralysis in one arm.

The second level of study was more cynical. Goebbels' Propaganda Ministry quoted the quatrains with monotonous regularity to 'prove' that Germany was destined to win the war and rule the world. Churchill responded by issuing a charming requisition demanding 'Astrologer, one, War Office for the use of' in order to discover what sort of esoteric advice the Nazis might be getting and before long, British Counter Intelligence had published its own 124-page book entitled *Nostradamus prophezeit den kriegsverlauf* ('Nostradamus prophesies the course of the war'). This book, brought out under the imprint of a genuine esoteric publisher and circulated throughout Germany in 1943, was packed with fictional predictions insisting only disaster lay ahead for the Nazis. But it is clear the authors used the real quatrains in preparing their propaganda version. Hitler is referred to as 'Hister' and in one verse it is predicted that he

Will be surprised at night by six men
Naked, without armour, [he will be] taken in his bed

As we have seen earlier, these are genuine lines, taken from Quatrain 30 of Century 3. But they refer to Captain de Montgomery, the man who killed King Henri in the joust, not to Hitler. Someone in Counter Intelligence could not quite suppress his British sense of humour, for the book loyally urges the Fuhrer to be especially vigilant and wear his wonderful body-armour while he slept.

Any reading of the prophecies soon convinces one that Nostradamus viewed the totality of the rise of Nazism and the course of the Second World War in detail. He certainly had no illusions about the outcome or the fate of the men who caused it. In Century 3, Quatrain 63 he wrote:

> The Roman's power will be totally broken
> After imitating the example of his great neighbour
> Occult hatreds and disputes
> Will push back the follies of these buffoons

The Roman was, of course, the posturing Benito Mussolini, who actually did well enough for Italy until he made the mistake of emulating his great neighbour, Hitler, and leading his country into the war. The French term 'occultes' in the original quatrain is translated simply as 'secret' by most commentators, even though it is perfectly obvious that it was the military might of the Allies which pushed back the two buffoons, not 'secret hatreds and disputes'. If, however, the word is translated directly as 'occult', which also means secret, but with esoteric connotations, the verse takes on a whole new dimension.

Once Hitler's occult interests are recognized, a great many of those actions which defy social or political explanation suddenly make sense. It has been argued, for example, that the deliberate flooding of the Berlin underground, with the subsequent death of thousands of Germans who used the system as an air raid shelter, was a lunatic blood sacrifice to the dark Teutonic gods in the hope that they would turn the tide to victory.

More to the point, there is evidence to suggest that Hitler's belief in a particularly crackpot occult theory[30] led to his insistence on sending his troops into Russia without proper winter equipment and also caused him to halt for a time the V2 rocket programme which might have won him the war. He was not alone in these peculiarities. Himmler wasted some of the finest minds in Germany on an investigation of the esoteric properties of the top hat worn at Eton and the bells of Oxford, which he believed were somehow deflecting the best efforts of the Luftwaffe. Hess made his famous flight to Scotland on the basis of a revelation which came to him in a dream. Even the persecution of the Jews, which did more than anything else to lose sympathy for the Nazi cause, was based on a distorted notion of Oriental esoteric doctrine. Occult hatreds and disputes did indeed play their part in pushing back the follies of these buffoons.

Eventually, of course, it all came tumbling down . . . and Nostradamus was there to chronicle the outcome. First he foresaw the end of Hitler:

> The fortress of those under siege
> Was cut into the depths by gunpowder
> The traitor will be entombed in it
> Never before was there so pitiful a schism among Germans

> Century 4, Quatrain 40

The last days of Hitler were spent more or less permanently in a concrete bunker sunk, by the use of explosives, under the grounds of the Berlin Chancellery. Strange though it might seem in retrospect, Germany remained united behind the Fuhrer right up to the last few weeks of the war. When it finally became clear to the Nazis that all was lost, the scheming and plotting would have done justice to a Byzantine Court. But it was plotting and scheming dissociated from reality. (One discussion centred on the negotiation of a pact between Nazi Germany and Great Britain to fight Russia – this at a time when the Allies were pressing into the suburbs of Berlin.) As Nostradamus said, never was there so pitiful a schism among Germans.

Hitler spent much of his time ordering the deployment of forces which had ceased to exist – his military staff were terrified to tell him how badly the war had gone – but was eventually forced to face reality. With only a few units of Hitler

Youth between the bunker and the approaching Allied soldiers, he married his long time mistress, Eva Braun, then poisoned her, his German Shepherd dog Blondi, and himself, thus fulfilling Nostradamus' prophecy that the bunker would be transformed into a tomb.

Nostradamus then went on to forecast the fate of the Nazis in the immediate aftermath of the war:

> Condemnation will be made of a great number
> When the leaders will be reconciled
> But one among them will be such bad news
> That they will not remain allies for long

Century 2, Quatrain 38

It is worth remembering that the war did not begin with the Allies in total harmony. Two major partners, America and the USSR, sought to stay outside the conflict altogether. It took the surprise attack on Pearl Harbour (which Nostradamus describes in Quatrain 100 of Century 9) to tilt US public opinion and Hitler's vicious attack on Russia to move Stalin. But as Nostradamus predicted, once the leaders were reconciled, world affairs began to take a very different turn.

And when the war was won, those on the defeated side were subjected, for the first time in modern history, to the judicial process of law, at the Nürmberg Trials where, again as Nostradamus forecast, many were condemned.

Yet the Allies did not remain allies for long. Stalin proved so intractable at the Yalta Conference, convened to lay the foundation of the post-war world, that Churchill actually suggested hostilities be resumed with a view to pushing the Soviets back behind their original borders. It might even have been an excellent idea, but the war-weary Americans would have none of it. The war was replaced by a Cold War which was destined to last almost fifty years.

# 13

# Modern Times

The modern era began, unheralded and almost totally unnoticed, in Germany in 1938. This was the year when Nazi scientists absolutely confirmed what physicists had long suspected – nuclear fission, the splitting of the atom to produce abundant energy, was a practical possibility. The German nuclear programme could not and did not remain secret for long. Refugee physicists were convinced it was only a matter of time before Hitler tried to build an atomic bomb. Hungarian-born physicists Leo Szilard, Eugene Wigner and Edward Teller prevailed upon Albert Einstein to address a letter to President Roosevelt. In late 1939 Roosevelt ordered the establishment of the Manhattan Project, an all-out effort to ensure that the Allies got there first.

The Project's second leader, General Leslie Groves of the Army Corps of Engineers, appointed theoretical physicist J. Robert Oppenheimer as director of the weapons laboratory built on an isolated mesa at Los Alamos, New Mexico. Working under the pressure of wartime urgency, physicists throughout the United States gradually cracked the problems associated with the production of fissionable material and in 1945, uranium-235 of bomb purity was shipped to Los Alamos, where it was fashioned into a gun-type weapon. In a barrel, one piece of uranium was fired at another, together forming a supercritical, explosive mass.

Another type of atomic bomb was also constructed using the

synthetic element plutonium. Enrico Fermi built a reactor at Chicago in late 1942, the prototype of five production reactors later erected at Hanford, Washington. These reactors manufactured plutonium by bombarding uranium-238 with neutrons. At Los Alamos the plutonium was surrounded with high explosives to compress it into a superdense, supercritical mass far faster than could be done in a gun barrel. The result was tested at Alamogordo, New Mexico, on July 16, 1945. It was the explosion of the world's first atomic bomb and it demonstrated a release of energy a million times greater than an equal weight of chemical high-explosive.

The scientists were far more confident about their gun-barrel bomb. No test was conducted, and the weapon was first employed in military action over Hiroshima, Japan, on August 6, 1945. The plutonium device was used to bomb Nagasaki three days later. Both cities were virtually destroyed, more than 100,000 people killed and a further 100,000 injured in what was unarguably the greatest man-made disaster in the whole of human history.

In Salon, four hundred years before, Nostradamus sought to make sense of the event within the framework of the knowledge of his day. He wrote:

Close by the harbours and within two cities
There will be two scourges beyond any ever seen
Hunger, plague, and people dispossessed by war
Will cry help from the great immortal God

Century 2, Quatrain 6

Both Hiroshima and Nagasaki were port cities and the bomb dropped on the latter was actually aimed at the harbour shipyards. Nostradamus wrote this vivid description of what happened when it struck:

As the sun rises, a great fire will be seen
Noise and light extending towards the north

Within the globe is death and screams
Death awaits through the weapon, fire and famine

Century 2, Quatrain 91

The massive death-toll following the explosions was more than matched by the number of injured survivors. All municipal services, including food supply, were utterly disrupted, so that half-starved men, women and children were a common sight.

But the most telling detail of all is the prophet's mention of plague in the first quoted quatrain. As a doctor, Nostradamus was all too familiar with the symptoms of plague – the suppurating sores, the swellings, the blackened faces and bodies . . . precisely the appearance presented by the victims of atomic bombing.

This was Nostradamus' first great prophecy of modern times, but certainly not his last. In Century 1, Quatrain 63 he gave an overview of the era:

After the pestilences have passed, the world grows small
And for a long time the lands of peace will be inhabited
People will move across the sky, the land and the sea with safety
Then wars will start again

This is a truly remarkable vision, with a multiplicity of layers. With improvements in medical practice, notably immunization techniques and the increasing development of new, more powerful antibiotics, many diseases which were once mass killers have now been virtually wiped out. Could these have been the pestilences Nostradamus meant . . . or was he referring to the man-made pestilences we have just been examining, at Hiroshima and Nagasaki? Either way, he certainly pinpointed one of the most striking characteristics of the modern era with his phrase 'the world grows small'.

For a man accustomed to travel only by horse or sail power

in a hazardous environment where the threat of brigandage or piracy was ever present, he must have been stunned by his visions of modern aeroplanes, cars, trains and iron ships – and the safety standards they achieved.

His reference to a long period of peace is less clear – since 1945, the world has endured a veritable litany of wars, several of them more destructive than the World Wars which have gone before.[31] But the prophecy is easier to understand when we remember Nostradamus' firmly Franco-centred viewpoint. Since its liberation from the Nazi jackboot and the establishment of the nuclear umbrella, France has endured a period of peace lasting more than half a century. This has not been totally uninterrupted, but overseas involvements in such countries as Vietnam and Algeria have been relatively minor; and none has resulted in an enemy on French soil. If this interpretation is correct, then Nostradamus predicts the peace will not last forever: and, indeed, there are specific prophecies of a fresh attack on France yet to come.

Nostradamus' preoccupation with France is again reflected in the curious Quatrain 33 of Century 9, where he wrote:

> Hercules, King of Rome, Hungary, Bohemia and Moravia
> Three times leader will be called De Gaulle
> Italy will tremble and the waters of St Mark
> The first above all kings to be honoured

There are aspects of this verse which present considerable difficulties, but the name de Gaulle rings down the centuries like a clarion.

Fame came to Charles de Gaulle during World War II. While other French military forces crumbled during the May 1940 German invasion, de Gaulle conducted one of the few successful tank operations. He was promoted to the position of Undersecretary of War on June 5 but fled the country when it become obvious that surrender was imminent. On June 18 he issued a radio appeal to the French nation to continue its resistance.

Although condemned to death by the Vichy Government, he persisted in building up Free French and resistance forces. In 1943 he formed a provisional government which took control of France after the Allied Normandy invasion of June 1944. As President of the provisional government from 1944 to 1946, de Gaulle worked with the Constituent Assembly to govern France and draw up a Constitution for the Fourth Republic, but disagreements with colleagues forced his resignation in January 1946. In 1958, when the Algerian War threatened to provoke civil war in France, de Gaulle was asked to form a government and became Premier on June 1. A new Constitution, which vested the president with strong executive powers, was approved by the electorate in September 1958, and de Gaulle was elected President of the Fifth Republic in December.

It was a career which absolutely fulfilled the prophecy made by Nostradamus centuries before. He was indeed three times leader: first as President of the Provisional Government, then as a President of the Fourth Republic and finally as the first President of the Fifth Republic. Until he finally fell foul of student unrest, his prestige, nationally and internationally, was enormous – higher by far than any king of France.

As Nostradamus watched the rise and fall of de Gaulle, he also noted the machinations of another great leader, this time of a country which was virtually terra incognita in his own day. In Century 8, Quatrain 92 he wrote:

> Distant from the kingdom, sent on a hazardous journey
> A great army he will hold and retain it for himself
> The leader will keep his subjects captive
> On his revolution, he will pillage the whole country

The place 'distant from the kingdom (of France)' was China. The hero of the quatrain was the remarkable Mao Tse-tung (Mao Zedong).

Mao Tse-tung was born on December 26, 1893, into a well-to-do peasant family in Shao-shan, Hunan province. As a child he worked in the fields and attended a local primary school, where he studied the traditional Confucian classics. By 1918, he had gone to Peking, where he worked briefly as a library assistant at Peking University. He did not attain regular student status, and neither did he master a foreign language or study abroad, unlike many of his classmates. In 1919, he returned to Hunan, where he engaged in radical political activity.

When the Chinese Communist party was organized in Shanghai in 1921, Mao was a founding member and leader of the Hunan branch. In 1927, General Chiang Kai-Shek reversed his party's policy of cooperation with the Communists. By the following year, he had purged all Communists from power. As a result, Mao was forced to flee to the countryside. The following year, a Chinese soviet was founded in Juichin, Kiangsi province, with Mao as chairman. Then the first of Nostradamus' predictions about Mao came true. A series of extermination campaigns by Chiang Kai-shek's Nationalist government forced him to abandon Juichin in October 1934 and begin the 'hazardous journey' that the history books now record as the Long March. And a long march it was. Remnants of the Communist forces reached Shensi in October 1935, after a journey of 10,000 km (6,000 miles). Mao retained personal control of the Red Army hardened by the rigours of the Long March and just over a decade later began the conflict which was to leave him leader of his country. The civil war of 1946 to 1949 saw the rapid defeat of Chiang's government, which was forced to flee to Taiwan. The People's Republic of China, formed by Mao in late 1949, was left in control of the entire Chinese mainland.

During the early 1950s, Mao served as chairman of the Communist party, chief of state, and chairman of the military commission. It soon became obvious that another of the Nostradamus' predictions was coming true with a vengeance, for Mao, as a leader, held his subjects captive in a way unparalleled even in the most repressive days of feudal China. He created communes which effectively destroyed the family structure of rural society, established a network of petty informers and sought to control not only the actions, but the very thoughts of his people through the introduction of a wide-ranging philosophy spelled out, in the manner of the Confucian analects, in his *Little Red Book*.

It was all outlined in a programme known as the Great Leap Forward, but the suddenness of the moves led to administrative confusion and popular resistance. As a consequence, Mao lost his position as chief of state and found his influence over the party severely weakened. During the 1960s, however, Mao made a comeback, and set in train the events which Nostradamus referred to in the final line of his prophecy. He called for a Great Proletarian Cultural Revolution and when he could not get his ideas across in the Peking Press, he used the Shanghai Press to attack the Peking leadership. Students, mobilized as Red Guards, became his most avid supporters. On a popular level the Cultural Revolution taught the Chinese masses that it was their privilege to criticize those in positions of authority and to take an active part in decision making. During the Revolution, Mao's *Little Red Book*, and buttons bearing his image were distributed to the masses, his word was treated as the ultimate authority on just about everything and he himself became the subject of a personality cult that must have been unique in its scope in human history. Outside of China, however, the Cultural Revolution was generally considered a frightening example of mass lunacy; and while the view was simplistic it proved, in the final analysis, to be largely correct. The result of Red Guard activity was to undermine many of the more important structures of the State and, more importantly, to leave an entire generation uneducated, untrained and generally unfit to take control with maturity. As Nostradamus had predicted, Mao pillaged the whole country.

There were other world leaders, of even more importance than Mao Tse-tung, who featured in this period of Nostradamus' visions. Notable among them was the 35th president of the United States, John Fitzgerald Kennedy. Kennedy was elected to office in 1961. At the age of 43, he was the youngest man and the first Roman Catholic ever to achieve the presidency. Rich, handsome and immensely popular, he seemed set for a brilliant presidential career. But Nostradamus thought otherwise:

> Before battle, the great one topples
> The great one to death, death too quickly and grieved
> Born imperfect: he goes the greater part
> Near the river of blood, the earth strained

Century 2, Quatrain 57

Cheetham considers this verse a prediction of the Cuban Missile Crisis which carried humanity to the very brink of nuclear war in 1962. The great one born imperfect she sees as Kennedy, who had a congenital back problem which troubled him most of his life and may also have seemed morally imperfect to Nostradamus because of his sexual peccadilloes. Kennedy's death, she argues, is predicted in line 2. There may actually be two 'great ones' referred to in this verse – the term is certainly used twice – and the second, who toppled largely because of his miscalculations in the Crisis, was Nikita Krushchev, the Soviet Premier. Either might reasonably be described as having gone the greater part of the way towards a war which would certainly have been a river of blood staining the earth for generations.

Nostradamus returned to John F. Kennedy and his dramatic death in this verse:

> The great one will fall in daytime from a thunderbolt
> An evil foretold by the bearer of a petition
> According to the presage, another is struck down at night
> When there is conflict in Reims, London and disease in Tuscany

Century 1, Quatrain 26

So it came about. Thinking ahead to the presidential campaign of 1964, Kennedy made an official visit to Texas in November 1963 in order to promote harmony between warring factions of the Democratic party there. While driving in a motorcade through Dallas on November 22, he was shot in the head, pitched forward like one struck down by a thunderbolt and died within an hour.

The evil had indeed been foretold, by the Washington society psychic, Jean Dixon, who actually wrote to White House contacts urging them to stop the Dallas trip. Mrs Dixon added to her reputation by predicting the further assassination of Kennedy's brother, Robert, who had held the post of Attorney General during his presidency.

Nostradamus presaged that Robert Kennedy would be struck down in the hours of darkness at an historical period when there was trouble in France and Britain. In 1968, student riots erupted in Paris and London. In the run-up to the US presidential election that same year, Robert Kennedy won the California primary. Minutes after his victory speech in the small hours of the morning, he was gunned down by Sirhan Sirhan and died in hospital a few days later.

President Lyndon B. Johnson appointed the Warren Commission to investigate the assassination of John F. Kennedy. In a massively unwieldy report that took years to prepare, the Commission concluded that the killer, acting alone, was 24-year-old Lee Harvey Oswald. Nostradamus was not so sure:

> Before the people, blood will be spilt
> From the sky it will not come
> But for a long time this will not be heard
> The spirit of one alone shall bear witness to it

Century 9, Quatrain 49

Kennedy's blood was spilt before the watching eyes of the huge crowds which had turned out to see the motorcade through

Dallas. According to the Warren Commission, the fatal shot came from above, fired by Oswald from a window in the high-rise book repository overlooking the scene – effectively from the sky. Not so, said Nostradamus, although it would be some time before anyone took issue with the official account. Experts did, nonetheless, eventually begin to take issue with the official account, suggesting that Oswald did not act alone, that the fatal shot came not from above, but from a grassy knoll by the side of the road as the parade was passing.

There was even, in final confirmation of the eerie prophecy, a suggestion that there was a single eye-witness, a man whose image appeared dimly in a blurred photograph of the grassy knoll at the time of the assassination.

Not all the prophet's predictions for the 1960s were quite so gloomy. In Quatrain 65 of Century 9, he forecast what was arguably the greatest technical achievement in the history of humanity:

To a corner of the moon he will be taken
Where he will walk on foreign soil
The unripe fruit will be the subject of great scandal
Great blame, but also great praise

America's Apollo space programme peaked in 1969. On July 20 of that year, the Apollo XI spacecraft ended a four-day flight with the first manned lunar landing. As Lieutenant Colonel Michael Collins orbited the Moon in the mother ship Columbia, Neil Armstrong and Colonel Edwin E. (Buzz) Aldrin, Jr touched down on a corner of the moon known as the Mare Tranquillitatis, or Sea of Tranquillity, in the Lunar Module Eagle. Armstrong was the first out – he jumped to the surface at 10.56pm and walked on the most foreign soil humanity had ever known.

Amazing though the achievement was, it became, as Nostradamus foresaw, the subject of controversy. America was deeply embroiled in the Vietnam War by this time and critics of the administration argued that American efforts could be better spent in seeking an end to the war, either by negotiation or by winning it outright. Other factions insisted sourly that the space race was a diversion from the serious business of politics and would bring no real benefits. But needless to say, the flood of praise that greeted the American achievement far outweighed the carping of the detractors.

As the Apollo moon programme neared its peak, space officials recognized that a reusable vehicle was necessary for continued large-scale operations. The Shuttle programme was formally authorized by President Richard Nixon on January 5, 1972.

The first launch, with Commander John Young and pilot Robert Crippen aboard, was made on April 12, 1981, with only minor problems. But the 25th mission – the tenth flight of the shuttle Challenger – ended less than two minutes after lift-off on January 28, 1986, when the large, external fuel tank exploded during ascent. The entire crew perished.

There are those who believe the disaster was foreseen by Nostradamus who wrote:

From the rest of humanity nine will be set apart
From judgment and advice separated
Their fate will be sealed at the moment of their departure
Kappa, Theta, Lambda dead, gone, scattered

> Century 1, Quatrain 81

There is no doubt that, of all professions, the crew of a spacecraft is the most isolated from the rest of humanity. The fate of those engaged in the 25th Challenger mission was indeed sealed at the moment of their departure from the ground – a 256-page report issued by a presidential commission of inquiry attributed the immediate cause of the disaster to the failure of an 'O' ring, a joint on one of the solid rocket boosters.

But if Nostradamus did watch the catastrophic launch, he

miscounted the crew – there were seven on board, not nine as predicted. The Greek terms kappa, theta, lambda are letters of the alphabet, equating to K, T or the sound Th, and L, and their use suggests the initials of those who perished. Here again, Nostradamus was in error. The Challenger crew consisted of Francis R. Scobee, pilot Michael J. Smith, Dr Judith A. Resnick, Lieutenant Colonel Ellison S. Onizuka, Dr Ronald E. McNair, Gregory B. Jarvis, and Christa McAuliffe, a high school teacher who had been chosen to become the first ordinary US citizen in space.

There is less controversy surrounding the prophetic predictions of other disasters which occurred in the 1980s. Some of his most chilling insights concerned Iran. The first portent of the troubles to befall that country in the present century is contained in Quatrain 70 of Century 1:

> Rain, hunger, conflict without respite in Iran
> Too great a trust will betray the Shah
> The end will begin in France
> A secret omen to be more moderate

Iran was an independent monarchy for more than 2,500 years until 1979 when the Shah, Muhammad Reza Pahlavi, was deposed and an Islamic republic was declared. The background to this development was accurately predicted by Nostradamus. In 1941 joint British-Soviet pressure forced the abdication of the allegedly pro-German Reza Shah. He was succeeded by his 22-year-old son. In the early 1950s the power of the new Shah was challenged by a nationalist leader and he was forced to flee the country briefly in 1953. He returned shortly with strong Western backing and emerged as a powerful and determined ruler. In 1963 he instituted the so-called White Revolution, an ambitious programme of modernization. The reforms appeared worthwhile enough on the surface – they included, among other aims, the emancipation of women – but they were accompanied by administrative corruption and a great deal of social disruption. In an attempt to keep order, the Shah came to rely increasingly on his secret police, the brutal Savak. It was, as Nostradamus said, a period of ceaseless conflict.

Towards the end of the 1970s, street riots led to the imposition of military rule. The Shah relied heavily on American military backing and ignored modern echoes of Nostradamus' call for him to be more moderate. Thus opposition continued unabated.

The end, as Nostradamus predicted, began in France. Some fifteen years before, the fundamentalist Islamic leader, Ayatollah Ruhollah Khomeini, had staged a series of demonstrations against the government. Khomeini was exiled to Iraq for his pains, but continued to work towards the overthrow of the Shah, first from Iraq, and later from Paris. Nostradamus wrote:

> His hand behind the bloody Alus
> Protection by sea is no longer guaranteed
> Between two rivers, the military hand is to be feared
> The black, angry man will make him repent
> Century 9, Quatrain 33

The term 'alus' is obscure, but I suspect it refers to the Shah's secret police whose activities, more than any other factor, led to his eventual downfall. Although Pahlavi was not aware of it at the time, Western support, symbolized by sea power, was no longer absolute – the popular unrest was becoming a real embarrassment to democratic America. The land between two rivers is Iraq, through which flow the Tigris and Euphrates. Nostradamus predicted – again accurately – a military threat from that quarter and at the same time hinted of the Ayatollah's activities before he went to live in France. There is no doubt at all that the 'black, angry man' destined to make the Shah repent was Khomeini himself, whose fulminations and black religious garb soon became a familiar image on the world stage.

The fulfilment of the prophecies rolled on relentlessly. On

January 6, 1979, the Shah lifted military rule and, a few days later, left the country. Khomeini returned to a tumultuous welcome on February 1, and on February 12 Iran was proclaimed an Islamic republic.

# 14
# Fate of Popes

Saint Malachy, known in his own day as Maelmaedoc ua Morgair, was a twelfth-century Irish bishop who reformed the church in Ireland. He was ordained in 1119, and served successively as Abbot of Bangor, Bishop of Connor, and Archbishop of Armagh, a position which made him Primate of Ireland. He reorganized the tribal hierarchies of the country, disciplined the clergy, established the Roman liturgy and introduced the Cistercian Order by founding the abbey of Mellifont. St Bernard of Clairvaux records, following an incident at Clonmel, 'the brethren knew that Malachy had the gift of prophecy'.

In 1138, he visited Rome and there fell into a profound trance in which he foresaw the succession of one hundred and twelve Popes from his own day until the final fall of the Church of Rome. When he awoke, he penned a predictive manuscript, in which he gave each Pope a Latin motto. Adrian IV, the only English Pope, who was born in St Albans (the 'white city') was, for example, given the appropriate motto De Rure Albo, 'from the white country'. Alexander IV, a former Cardinal of Ostia, was referred to as Signum Ostiense. Clement XIII, one-time Governor of Umbria, was called Rosa Umbriae. And so on.

The manuscript was forwarded to the Vatican where it lay in the secret archives until 1590, nearly a quarter of a century after the death of Nostradamus. But while there could have been no question of plagiarism, several prophecies made by

Nostradamus about the fate of the Papacy are uncomfortably close to the predictions of Malachy, whose work suggests that after the present Pope, John Paul II, there will be only two more before the entire institution is swept away.

In the twentieth century, Malachy named Benedict XV, who reigned during World War I in which millions died, Religio Depopulata, the 'depopulation of religion'. Pius XII, who ruled the Vatican from 1939 to 1958, was Pastor Angelicus, or 'angelic shepherd'. He was succeeded by John XXIII, a former Archbishop of Venice, the city of the sea, who navigated the Church into entirely new waters. Malachy referred to him as Pastor et Nauta, 'shepherd and navigator'.

John was followed, four years later, by Paul VI, Flos Florum or 'flower of flowers', possibly reflecting the floral motif on his coat of arms. From that point, Malachy foresaw only four more Popes: De Meditate Lunae, 'from the middle (half) of the moon', De Labore Solis, 'the labour of the sun', Gloria Olivae 'glory of the olive tree' and Petrus Romanus, 'Peter of Rome'.

As well as many earlier Popes, Nostradamus pinpointed both John XXIII and his successor with these words:

> Four years the seat of power will be held to some little good
> The one who follows will be libidinous in life
> Ravenna and Pisa, Verona will give support
> To see the cross of the Pope elevated

Century 6, Quatrain 26

And again:

> On the passing of an elderly Pope
> There will be elected a Roman of good age
> Who, it will be said, weakens the seat
> And long held with great effort

Century 5, Quatrain 56

In Century 6, Quatrain 20, he speaks of John XXIII alone:

The false union will last a short time
With the greater part of the reforms a few changes
In the vessels there will be great suffering
When Rome has a new leopard

The clue to identity lies in the term 'leopard' – John XXIII had a winged leopard on his coat of arms. Although he was already 77 years old when he came to office, he held the seat of power for over four years and the verdict of history has been that he was an extraordinarily good man, who made valiant attempts to reform the Church.

But as Nostradamus remarks, little enough good came from his tenure and the inertia of the institution ensured that the greater part of his reforms eventually amounted to relatively few changes. The 'false union' may refer to the ecumenical movement which, though it is still paid considerable lip service, was never really established in any practical way.

The use of the term 'vessels' in this quatrain is particularly interesting and may have an extremely subtle and convoluted meaning. Given the historical anti-feminist stance of the Church, Nostradamus, hopefully with tongue in cheek, may have used 'vessels' as a shortening of 'vessels of iniquity', an age-old misogynistic description of women. If so, the line fits remarkably well since the hopes of a more liberal attitude towards women, which flowered during John XXIII's papacy, died with him.

John XXIII held office for something more than four years and was succeeded by Paul VI. According to Erika Cheetham, he was widely reputed to have had a homosexual lover, a rumour which, if true, would certainly account for Nostradamus' comment about his 'libidinous life'.

Pope John was an elderly man when he died and Paul, when he took office, was, as Nostradamus remarked, 'a good age'. Although he held onto the papacy for quite a long time – some fifteen years from 1963 to 1978 – it was not without effort for, as predicted, he weakened the prestige and authority of his office. The main problem that arose during his reign was the Sindona affair.

Paul VI was friendly with Michele Sindona, a Sicilian banker who was eventually accused of having Mafia connections. During his term of office Sindona was appointed adviser to the Vatican Bank. When one of his own banks, the Banco Ambrosiano, came close to collapse in 1982, a whole network of financial corruption was suddenly brought to light. The Press had a field day, although the full extent of Vatican involvement was never fully revealed.

> Paul the celibate will die three leagues from Rome
> While the two nearest flee the destroyer
> When Mars will be the most terrible influence
> Of the cock and the eagle of France, the three brothers

Century 8, Quatrain 46

Although this is not the easiest quatrain Nostradamus ever wrote, the reference to Mars suggests a time of war; and while wars are not difficult to find in the present era, this one gave concern to France and America (symbolized by the eagle) in particular. This would suggest the Iran-Iraq war, which erupted on September 22, 1980, when Iraq invaded Iran. This war was certainly bloody enough to justify the Nostradamus comment about Mars as the most terrible influence. In June 1982, faced with strong Iranian resistance, Iraq withdrew its troops from most parts of Iran and Iran launched several massive human wave attacks. From that point, the war settled into a long-drawn-out stalemate with the death toll running into millions. The strong US and French links were increasingly highlighted after 1984 when Iraq began attacks on Gulf shipping. This strategy helped draw other countries into the conflict to increase pressure on Iran to accept a negotiated settlement. In response, Iran attacked ships carrying war material to Iraq and those belonging to countries that helped Iraq. Iraq purchased arms mainly from France and the USSR. The United States, officially neutral in the conflict, gave non-military aid and intelligence information to Iraq. In 1985 and 1986 it secretly supplied small amounts of arms to Iran in the hope of improving relations. In May 1987, after the US frigate Stark was hit by an Iraqi missile in what appeared to be an accident, the United States decided to increase its naval presence in the Gulf and allow 11 Kuwaiti tankers to fly the US flag. The decision led to various confrontations with Iranian vessels.

The reference to those nearest 'fleeing the destroyer' may actually be associated with the Kurdish and Shi'ite minorities in Iraq who had problems with the Hussein government throughout the Iran-Iraq War and its immediate aftermath, even though it took another Gulf War for their plight to be highlighted in the world Press.

All these clues suggest a particular timing which would mean the celibate Paul in the first line of the verse was Paul VI. By now it may come as no surprise to learn that the Pope's villa, where he died in 1978 as tensions between Iran and Iraq were just beginning to build, was the exact distance from Rome that Nostradamus predicted.

The prophet looked to the next incumbent of the See of Peter in this ominous verse:

When the sepulchre of the great Roman is found
The day after will be elected a Pope
By his Senate he will not be approved
Poisoned is his blood by the sacred chalice

Century 3, Quatrain 65

When white smoke finally emerged from the Conclave chimney and the Cardinals made their traditional announcement, 'Habemus Papem' ('We have a Pope') the new man proved a total surprise to almost every informed Vatican watcher. His name was Albino Luciani and as Patriarch of Venice from 1970, he had not played a prominent role in international church affairs before his election. This was the man to whom Malachy assigned the motto, De Meditate Lunae, 'from the middle (or half) of the moon'. By an odd coincidence, he was destined to survive only a little more than a lunar month.

Luciani took the papal name of John Paul I and showed himself at once as an informal man interested in reform. He abandoned the traditional coronation ceremony with the triple tiara and substituted a much more simple investiture with the pallium (a white woollen stole-like band), to symbolize the pastoral nature of the papal office. He insisted on walking, rather than being carried on the ornate throne normally used and his first speech shocked traditionalists by avoiding the use of the royal 'we' when referring to himself.

John Paul became Pope on August 26, 1978. There is no recorded instance of a great Roman sepulchre being discovered the day before, although a tomb which some experts believed might be the actual grave of St Peter was found the following year. All the same, John Paul's actions soon earned him the disapproval of his 'Senate', the Curia. He set the ball rolling with a speech in which he remarked that God was not only the Heavenly Father, but the Heavenly Mother as well. He began openly to support women's rights and even agreed to meet a US Congressional delegation to discuss artificial birth control. These were troubled waters indeed, but worse was to come. Early in September, he asked Cardinal Jean Villot, his Secretary of State, to begin an investigation into the affairs of the Vatican Bank. On September 28, the iconoclastic Pope went further. He handed Villot a list he had drawn up of individuals suspected of belonging to the secret Freemason's Lodge known as P2. All on the list, he instructed, were to be transferred, reassigned, or asked to resign. Had his instructions been carried out, the repercussions for the Vatican power structure would have been profound. But his instructions were not carried out. He dined with his Cardinals and the following morning was found dead in his bed. At least one contemporary author suspected foul play. So, it seems, did Nostradamus:

> He who will have government of the Great Cape
> Will be led to take action
> The twelve Red Ones will come to spoil the cover
> Under murder, murder will come to be done

Century 4, Quatrain 11

Was John Paul I handed a poisoned chalice, as the prophet suggests in the earlier quatrain? Certainly the circumstances surrounding his death raised far more questions than they should. Investigators have asked why, for example, Cardinal Villot released false information about the situation to the Press, why no inquest was held on a 66-year-old man apparently in excellent health and why, above all, the body was cremated, against strict Catholic custom, in what some considered to be indecent haste?

Whatever about the poisoned chalice, there was certainly murder upon murder following his death, each linked with precisely those areas John Paul wished investigated.

On January 21, 1979, Judge Emilio Alessandrini was murdered while investigating the activities of the Banco Ambrosiano.

On March 20, 1979, Mino Pecorelli, an investigative journalist, was murdered while publishing a series of articles on the Masonic Lodge P2.

On July 11, Giorgio Ambrosioli was murdered following his testimony to law enforcement agencies about Michele Sindona, Banco Ambrosiano director Roberto Calvi and Bishop Paul Marcinkus of the Vatican Bank.

On July 13, 1979, Lieutenant Colonel Antonio Varisco, head of the Rome Security Service, was murdered while investigating the activities of Masonic Lodge P2.

On July 21, 1979, Boris Guiliano, head of the Palermo CID, was murdered while investigating allegations that Michele

Sindona had used the Vatican Bank to 'launder' Mafia money.

Alongside the murders, there were several more mysterious deaths. Graziella Corrcher, Roberto Calvi's secretary, fell from a fourth floor window in the Banco Ambrosiano and died on June 17, 1982. Calvi himself was found hanging from a bridge in London on the same day. On October 2, Guiseppe Dellacha, a Banco Ambrosiano executive, died from a fall from the bank window. Finally, on March 23, 1986, Michele Sindona was found poisoned in an Italian jail.

It was all quite remarkable, as were Vatican refusal, early in 1980, to provide videotaped depositions on behalf of Sindona during his trial in the United States; the letters of comfort issued by the Vatican taking responsibility for more than $1 billion worth of debts contracted by Calvi's banks; and the refusal of the Vatican to acknowledge a shareholders' letter outlining details of the links between the Vatican Bank, the P2 Masonic Lodge, Calvi and the Mafia.

Nostradamus made several perceptive comments on the whole affair in Quatrain 9 of Century 6:

> In the sacred temples, there will be made scandals
> They will be thought of as honours and praiseworthy matters
> By one who they mark for silver, gold and coins
> The end will be torments very strange

The sacred temples were those of Rome, the scandals, as shown in the third line, financial. At first, everything appeared honourable and above board: what could be more respectable than a bank, and a Vatican-backed bank at that? But as we have seen, it ended in 'torments' that were very strange indeed.

By this time, of course, Sindona's friend Paul VI and the ill-fated John Paul I were both well out of the picture. Their place as Vicar of Christ had been taken by Karol Josef Wojtyla, the first non-Italian Pope since the days of Nostradamus and the first Polish Pope ever. Cardinal Wojtyla, who took the name John Paul II, was elected on October 16, 1978. As always,

Nostradamus saw him coming:

Not from Spain, but from ancient France
He will be elected from the trembling ship
To the enemy he will make assurance
Who in his reign will be a cruel blight

Century 5, Quatrain 49

At the time of his election, there was much talk of the possibility of a South American Pope – an area which in Nostradamus' time was under the sovereignty of Spain. So, 'not from Spain' was a reasonable prediction. So too, curiously enough, was the remainder of the first line. The son of a Polish army officer, Karol Wojtyla was born in Wadowice, south western Poland, which in ancient times was actually French territory since it came within the boundaries of Charlemagne's empire.

The ship of the Church was trembling indeed at the time he came to power, as even the highly abbreviated account of the Sindona affair given above clearly indicates. The remainder of the prediction is equally clear and accurate. As a Pole, John Paul II knew instinctively who his great enemy was – the Soviet authorities who bolstered Poland's long discredited Communist government.

He came to power some years before the collapse of Communism in Eastern Europe, at a time when the Cold War was still chill. Memories of the Russian invasion of Hungary and Czechoslovakia's short-lived Prague Spring were still vivid. Against this background, developments in Poland took on a distinctly ominous tinge.

Strange developments they were. After a series of strikes against food price increases in July and August, 1980, the Polish government agreed to a list of demands presented by a strikers' committee headed by Lech Walesa, an electrician from the Gdansk shipyards. The demands did not stop at wage increases, but asked for price reductions, the right to strike and form independent unions, curtailment of censorship, greater religious freedom, and the release of political prisoners. On September 17, 1980, representatives of 3,000,000 Polish workers met in Gdansk and established the Solidarity labour federation, the first free trade union in any Communist country. Walesa became its chairman. Over the next few months Solidarity members engaged in strikes and demanded further reforms. Rural Solidarity, an independent farmers' union, was organized in April 1981. At a national congress in September 1981, Solidarity declared itself a 'social movement' and demanded free elections. Throughout the autumn of 1981 fears mounted that the USSR would intervene to stop what appeared to be a threat to Communist rule in Poland. There were Soviet troop movements on the Polish border and it seemed only a matter of days, perhaps even hours, before the Kremlin ordered an invasion. At this point, according to sources close to the Vatican, John Paul II made the assurance to the enemy that Nostradamus had predicted. He sent a secret message to the Soviet leadership promising that if an invasion was mounted, he would fly at once to Warsaw and stand, in full papal regalia, before the approaching tanks. The world-wide political repercussions of such a threat were too much for the Kremlin. Any thought of invasion was dropped and more subtle measures adopted. On December 13, Premier Wojciech Jaruzelski imposed martial law and arrested the union's leaders. Most worker resistance to the martial-law regime was ended by the beginning of 1982, and Solidarity was officially abolished the following October.[32]

Although John Paul was successful in that instance, the enemy remained, as Nostradamus predicted, a cruel blight. In December 1979, just over a year after his election to the papacy, the USSR intervened militarily in Afghanistan, provoking the most serious international crisis of the decade. A bare seven years later, United Nations human rights officials reported that 10,000 to 12,000 Afghan civilians had been killed in the previous nine months by Soviet and Afghan government forces, and that children had been killed by the indiscriminate use of explosives disguised as toys. The continuation of military action, they concluded, would lead to a situation 'approaching genocide'. John Paul II had personal dangers to worry about as well, as Nostradamus clearly predicted in Century 10, Quatrain 65:

Oh great Rome, your ruin comes close
Not of your walls, but of your blood and substance
The sharp one of letters will be so horrible a notch
Pointed steel placed up his sleeve, ready to wound

This suggests an attempt to strike at Rome not by military attack, but through an assassination attempt on the Pope. And there was indeed an attempt on John Paul II's life by Mehmet Ali Agca, a bizarre Turkish terrorist, who later claimed to be a reincarnation of Jesus Christ. In actuality, he was the son of a miner. He attended the universities of Ankara and Istanbul and in 1979 was charged with the murder of Abdi Ipekci, editor of the left-wing Turkish newspaper Milliyet. He escaped during his trial and reportedly threatened to kill Pope John Paul II during a papal visit to Turkey. He subsequently fled abroad, and on May 13, 1981, shot and wounded the Pope and two bystanders while the pontiff was greeting pilgrims in Saint Peter's square. Agca was sentenced to life imprisonment by an Italian court, but his motivation remained a subject of controversy. Turkish authorities identified him as a member of the right-wing National Movement party, but he claimed to be connected with the Popular Front for the Liberation of Palestine, who, however, denied any knowledge of him. He later told police that he had acted with the help of Bulgarian agents. This led to speculation that the Bulgarian Secret Service might have backed the assassination attempt on KGB prompting because of Soviet concern over the Pope's encouragement of Solidarity.

The only trouble with all this is that it does not fit the
Nostradamus verse at all. Was the prophet mistaken? Perhaps
not, for there was a second, much less publicized, attempt on
the Pope's life. This occurred during a State visit to Portugal
in 1982, when one of his entourage, a priest (a 'man of letters'
according to the prediction) tried to stab him with a long knife
he had hidden up his sleeve.

# 15

# The End of the World

By now, it should be obvious that Nostradamus must be taken very seriously as a prophet. From his own day to the present time he has again and again shown himself capable of foreseeing the future both in broad perspective and specific detail. While a great number of his verses are obscure, many others clearly name places, a few name people and some even give precise dates. In these circumstances, it makes good sense to try to find out what Nostradamus has to say about the future of our modern world.

This is not quite as straightforward as it seems. Prophecies are always easier to interpret in hindsight, and beyond that, not every published source of the Nostradamus predictions is wholly reliable: some authors, in their enthusiasm, produce untenable interpretations. John Hogue, for example, translates Quatrain 31 of Century 10 as:

The Russians will enter Afghanistan
The Moslems will find these areas open
The Afghans would like to keep Afghanistan
But the resistance will be buried[33]

If this interpretation was accurate, it would point towards one of the clearest prophecies Nostradamus ever made. Unfortunately this is not the case at all. In the original, the quatrain reads:

Le saint empire viendra en Germanie
Ismaelites trouveront lieux ouverts
Anes voudront aussi la Carmanie
Les soustenens de terre tous couverts

Even those unfamiliar with medieval French might wonder what terms were translated as 'Russians', 'Afghans' and 'Afghanistan'. A closer, if far less exciting, interpretation might read:

The holy empire will come to Germany
The Ishmaelites will find their openings
The asses will also wish for Carmania
The supporters of the ground are all covered

What this predicts I have no idea,[34] but it clearly does not refer to the Russian invasion of Afghanistan.

The point made is far from academic. As we approach the year 2000, there is increasing interest in prophecy in general and, in particular, the prophecies of Nostradamus. It is an uneasy interest, for it rests on a sort of instinctive millennarianism. Millennarianism is defined as any religious movement that prophesies the imminent destruction of the present order and the establishment of a new one. It is closely related to the ideas of 'last days' and 'final judgment' found in Judaism, Christianity, Islam, and Zoroastrianism. Christian millennarian beliefs were derived from Jewish apocalyptic traditions current in the centuries before and after Jesus Christ. The New Testament employs the imagery of Jewish apocalyptic literature, but centres on the expectation that Christ 'will come again with glory to judge both the quick and the dead'. Apocalyptic literature itself describes the end period of world history, and depicts the final confrontation between God and the powers of evil. The conflict frequently culminates in a world catastrophe.

It is fairly easy to be sanguine about such matters so long as they are projected into a distant future. Once they come closer, they make people nervous. In Christian tradition, the most likely time for the world to end is the conclusion of a millennium, or thousand year period, measured from the birth of Christ. There was panic throughout Europe as the clock approached midnight on the last day of AD999 and it would require a dedicated optimist to suggest that humanity has evolved so far as to rule out any repetition in 1999.

The process has, in fact, already begun. Fundamentalist preachers and biblical scholars frequently quote the New Testament Book of Revelation or the Old Testament Book of Daniel to support their thesis that the 'last days' are upon us. [35] In their remarkable work, *The Messianic Legacy*, [36] authors Michael Baigent, Richard Leigh and Henry Lincoln sum up the doctrine neatly:

> For the fundamentalist, the world has entered the Last Days, just as it was believed to have done in Jesus' time. The Antichrist will shortly appear (if he has not already done so) and wreak assorted kinds of havoc. A period of 'tribulation' will ensue, culminating in the epic Battle of Armageddon and the world will be destroyed in some kind of holocaust. After this débâcle, the Second Coming will occur – Jesus will descend in glory from the heavens, the dead will rise from their graves and the new Kingdom will be inaugurated.

But as Baigent, Leigh and Lincoln point out, the contemporary interpretation of the doctrine does not end there. Specifics are dragged in. The Antichrist is often identified with the Soviet Union, Saddam Hussein, or any other current political enemy. Their analysis of doctrines propounded by one of America's most powerful fundamentalist religious organizations produces this curious picture:

> [The organization] . . . identifies the menacing ten-crowned 'Beast' of the Book of Revelation – that is, the Antichrist – quite precisely as the EEC . . . It is predicted that the nations of the EEC

will wage war against the United States and the United Kingdom, will defeat them and will then enslave them. Britain and America will become satellites of a new world power based in Europe and this power will embark on the Third World War, presumably against the Soviet Union.

Biblical prophecies are invoked to forecast that the war will last two and a half years and cost the lives of two thirds of the population of Britain and America . . . 'In this fearful, awesome atomic age, World War III will start with nuclear devastation, unleashed on London, Birmingham, Manchester, Liverpool, New York, Washington, Philadelphia, Detroit, Chicago, Pittsburg without warning!'

At the end of the Third World War, the climactic Battle of Armageddon will be fought somewhere in the Middle East. The Antichrist will appear again . . . and contend against the forces of God . . . God's forces, commanded by Jesus . . . will naturally emerge triumphant . . .

One disturbing thesis of *The Messianic Legacy* is that such predictions, if believed by politicians and others in positions of power, could become self-fulfilling:

> . . . an extraordinary and ever increasing number of people in America today take them quite seriously and are not only resigned to an imminent apocalypse, but actually, in some sense, look forward to it, in expectation of a blissful eternity in the millennial Kingdom of the Second Coming. Among this number, it has been suggested, is the President of the United States.

The President referred to was Ronald Reagan, now retired, but since there is no bar against fundamentalist beliefs in the White House, journalist Ronnie Dugger's concern, expressed in *The Guardian*, remains always current: 'If a crisis arises in the Middle East and threatens to become a nuclear confrontation, might President Reagan be predisposed to believe that he sees Armageddon coming and that this is the will of God?'

Professor John Kessel of North Carolina State University, is among those who have highlighted the inconsistencies in apocalyptic theory. Kessel majors on the fact that if we are to take it seriously, we must first relegate God Almighty to the extraordinary position of a male chauvinist pig. In a powerful fictional account of the supposed 'last days'[37] he writes:

And now, this very evening, Lucy was invited to watch these men usher in the Millennium that other men had predicted every fifty years for the last two thousand years of man-ruled history. A Millennium ruled by the male God, who had created the universe for the benefit of man. This male God would send his son, the Prince of Peace, to slaughter his male enemies and run the world for a thousand years.

Those who did not accept the truth of Revelation would depart, cursed, to an everlasting fire ruled by a male Satan, who in these last terrible days before the Second Coming was attempting to pervert as many believers as possible by means of the male Antichrist.

Where did women fit in? Where else: they took their accustomed roles as worthy followers, innocent victims, or damned unbelievers. And oh yes – as temptresses, Satan's agents were often female. Indeed, one of the signs that the Millennium was imminent was that women had not been keeping their place.

And all that massive machinery of history had been set in motion because the first woman, created by the male God to serve man in the Garden of Eden, was too stupid or too contrary – male theologians had debated this point down through the ages – to follow instructions. And her husband, who ought to have known better than to listen to her, had followed his dick into perdition.

Unfortunately, not everyone displays the common sense of a Professor Kessel. Where Revelation or Daniel are not quoted to support apocalyptic theory, Nostradamus often is. One of the most widespread convictions among those who have not studied the quatrains – and even some who have – is that he predicted a nuclear Third World War followed by the end of the world in 1999. The trend is illustrated by current interpretation of

Century 2, Quatrain 5:

> When in a fish, letters and documents are enclosed
> From out of it will come one who will then make war
> Far across the sea his fleet will have travelled
> Approaching near the Italian shore

Most contemporary experts consider that the 'fish' in this quatrain is a submarine and suggest that the verse predicts a Third World War with Arab forces striking at the 'soft underbelly' of Europe. A less apocalyptic mindset quickly produces a very different picture.

The mention of the Italian shoreline implies that the fleet referred to is heading into the Mediterranean. The letters and documents in the submarine suggest sealed orders. There is certainly an attack, but the attack is not on Italy – the fleet only approaches the Italian coast and, having travelled a great distance to get to its destination, cannot have originated in the Middle East, which is relatively close. In fact, the fleet in question is most likely to have been the US Sixth Fleet, which did sail some distance to reach the Mediterranean in 1986. Putting all the clues together, we have a quatrain which points quite clearly to President Reagan's carrier-based attack on Libya in that year. Another quatrain generally interpreted in apocalyptic terms is:

> The Oriental one will come from his seat of power
> Passing over the Apennines to see France
> He will cross the sky, the waters and snow
> And all he will strike with his rod

Century 2, Quatrain 29

The Oriental one, or 'man from the East' (usually rendered Middle East since it suits the apocalyptic picture better than Asia) is taken as the notorious 'Third Antichrist' and his movement across the Apennines is held to mark the start of World War Three.

Although there is little doubt this is a verse which relates to the modern era – the reference to flight in line three establishes the broad dating – it is difficult to see where the rest comes from. The quatrain clearly says this Oriental flies in to see France, not to attack it. The only hint of aggression is contained in the last line, but this is certainly personal and may actually be symbolic.

Taken as a whole, it would seem to me that far from predicting the Third Antichrist sometime in our future, this quatrain refers to something in our immediate past – the development of the Transcendental Meditation Movement in the 1960s. The Oriental was, of course, the Maharishi, who came from his seat of power in the Himalayas and settled briefly in France. The third line, which describes his journey, includes the word 'snow', a rare commodity in the Middle East, but a dominant characteristic of the great Asiatic mountain chain. If, as I suspect, the reference to the rod should be read symbolically, then it surely points towards the blows the Maharishi struck against the smug materialism of established religion with his insistence on a spiritual dimension which could be explored by the individual. Whether or not one is a follower of the Maharishi, it is difficult to deny his impact on the thinking of the Sixties, particularly among the young, particularly when the Beatles took him as their guru.[38]

Sometimes the experts might be excused for their tendency towards apocalyptic interpretations, as in this quatrain:

One who the infernal gods of Hannibal
Will cause to rise, terrifying humanity
Never greater horror was told in the papers
Than will come to the Romans through Babel

.                                          Century 2, Quatrain 30

Hannibal was a North African general who terrified Rome during the Second Punic War (218-201 BC) so it is clear that the first line of the verse refers to the gods of war. The mention of newspapers in line three plainly makes this a modern prophecy. But does it really refer to World War Three as most commentators suggest?

There is, in fact, a set of historical circumstances which fits the facts rather better. The one who raised the gods of war and terrified humanity was Hitler. He had a close relationship with the Italian leader Mussolini, but the Italian people (the 'Romans') were far less happy with this development than their leader, especially after the outbreak of World War II when the morale of the Italian armed forces sank so low that they gained a reputation for incompetence which has lasted to this day. [39]

Towards the end of the war, the Italians had had enough. They overthrew the Fascist regime and imprisoned their former leader. Then, through the babel of propaganda characteristic of wartime, came the worst news the Romans could possibly have received. The monster Hitler had invaded the north of the country (exactly as Hannibal did in 218 BC), freed Mussolini and established a puppet regime with Il Duce at its head. Difficult days for the Italians, but not, as it transpired, the end of the world. A very similar situation has arisen with this quatrain:

> After the great human misery, an even greater approaches
> The great cycle of the centuries renewed
> Rain, blood, milk, hunger, war and pestilence
> In the sky will be seen a fire, followed by a tongue of sparks

Century 2, Quatrain 46

Although many Nostradamus students see in it a description of the last days, a calmer interpretation might see World War I, the 'great human misery' which was immediately followed by 'an even greater' – the influenza epidemic which cost more lives than the war itself. Nostradamus specifically describes the rain-sodden bloody, hungry trench war as followed by pestilence in the third line. The final line is a clear description of mortar shells exploding in the night sky.

The apocalyptic interpretation appears yet again in connection with this verse:

> The incredible army will leave Europe
> And join up close to the submerged island
> The NATO fleet folds its standard
> At the navel of the world a greater voice is substituted

> Century 2, Quatrain 22

Here too, most modern interpreters read the quatrain as predicting the start of Armageddon. But if so, it has already been and gone. The navel of the world is the Middle East, the ancient birthplace of civilization. The 'incredible army' which left Europe (and elsewhere, notably America if my interpretation is correct) was a cooperative international effort previously thought to have been impossible, due to European rivalries and the machinations of the Cold War. NATO folded its standard, amid some criticism, because its charter did not permit it to intervene in a dispute beyond the boundaries of Europe. And in the Middle East a greater voice – that of the United Nations – was substituted. Not Armageddon at all, although there were those who thought it might be at the time, but rather the Allied strike on Iraq following that country's annexation of Kuwait. How easily the apocalyptic viewpoint can distort an interpretation. A complication arises here. There seems to be little doubt that Nostradamus himself was attracted towards apocalyptic doctrines and must have known the theory that the world would end with the Second Coming in or around the year 2000. David Pitt Francis argues convincingly[40] that several quatrains were profoundly influenced by biblical prophecy. As we have already seen, like many of his contemporaries, he subscribed to ideas of an Antichrist.

But for all of his Roman Catholic beliefs, the prophet of Salon could not quite bring himself to abandon his personal visions. And while many of those relating to the modern era were dark and frightening, there is little in the quatrains to suggest a third global war, nuclear or otherwise. Furthermore, it is possible to state categorically that Nostradamus did not forecast the end of the world in 1999 or any other imminent date, if for no other reason than that his prophecies extend far beyond the present age into a future that stretches at least to the year AD 7000.

> Twenty years of the moon's reign pass
> Seven thousand years another monarch shall hold
> When the sun takes up his days
> Then shall my prophecies be complete
>
> Century 1, Quatrain 48

But if Nostradamus did not forecast apocalypse now, what did he prophesy for the rest of the twentieth century and beyond? The remainder of the present book is an attempt to answer that question. But before plunging into what must be a fascinating analysis, a few words of caution are appropriate.

There can be no question that everyone who studies the prophecies of Nostradamus interprets them in accordance with his or her own prejudices. Close examination of the available literature brings to light another phenomenon: contemporary political events are invariably reflected as well.

Take the frequently-quoted verse:

> One day there will be friendship between two great leaders
> Their great power will be seen to grow
> The new world will be at its peak of power
> To him of blood, the number is reported
>
> Century 2, Quatrain 89

Almost every recent commentary suggests the 'two great leaders' are the Presidents of the United States and the Soviet Union, specifically US President Ronald Reagan, during his terms of office, and Soviet Premier Mikhail Gorbachev.

This interpretation is extremely convincing. After decades of Cold War, the world watched in amazement as a friendly relationship between these two unlikely comrades grew out of a series of summit meetings, mainly convened to discuss arms control.

As their friendship increased, so too did their power, since cooperation between their countries meant they could now bring about movement in many areas which had been stalemated for years. The 'new world' (America) became the only real superpower, following the collapse of the Communist system in Eastern Europe, and in this sense has reached the peak of its power. The birthmark on Gorbachev's forehead, which looks like a bloodstain, indicates he is the 'man of blood' mentioned in the quatrain; and to him is reported the number of missiles and other armaments involved in the historic arms limitation negotiations.

Convincing indeed; and it may even be accurate. But commentators on Nostradamus in the decades around the Second World War were equally adamant that the two great leaders must be Hitler and Mussolini.

Once again the friendship seemed unlikely. Italy fought against Germany in World War I, a position Mussolini had personally supported. Once again, when they got together, their power was seen to grow as the influence of Fascism spread. It could even be argued that it is more realistic to claim America was at the peak of its power in that era rather than today. Now, the USA is a military superpower only – its position as the pre-eminent economic superpower has been overtaken by Japan. During World War II, it was at its peak both militarily and economically, the strongest nation, by whatever measure, in the world.

The 'man of blood', in this interpretation, was, of course,

Adolf Hitler, on whose hands was the blood of millions, notably that of the Jews. And it was the number of Jews exterminated in the death camps during the notorious 'Final Solution' which was reported to him.

It must be fairly obvious from this comparison that which interpretation you elect to believe is largely a matter of personal choice – the evidence is equally strong on both sides. But selecting the first interpretation has far-reaching implications. Those who back the Reagan-Gorbachev theory interpret other quatrains to suggest the friendship will not last, that both superpowers will become embroiled in a Middle Eastern war which will eventually go nuclear and that the world will be destroyed in a final apocalyptic conflagration around the turn of the millennium.

This overall interpretation is now so widely accepted[41] that it comes as something of a surprise to discover how little evidence there is for it in the works of Nostradamus himself; and how many quatrains actively contradict it. The *Centuries*, it must be remembered, do not form a coherent future history, but are rather a series of disconnected cameos in which a verse on General Franco may be followed by a prophecy about the French Revolution. Thus any broad picture must necessarily be selective and consequently reflects the mindset of the selector.

In these circumstances, I have resisted the temptation of adding my own theories to an already overflowing melting-pot by outlining any integrated picture of our immediate future as forecast by Nostradamus. Instead, I propose to select, in the order of their original publication, those verses which seem to me to relate to the late twentieth century, the twenty-first century and beyond.

As you read them, any picture of the years ahead will be of your own extraction and not a vision imposed upon you by the prejudices of interpretation. Of course, you may, by the time you have finished this book, agree whole-heartedly with the latter-day visionaries of impending apocalypse. But I doubt it.

# 16

# Visions of the Future

Nine of the ten Nostradamus *Centuries* contain one hundred four-line verses. Most, but not all, appear to be predictions.[42] The language in which they are written is difficult – a melange of medieval French, Latin, Greek and a smattering of other tongues. Because of this and the anagrams, ciphers and codes Nostradamus added, many admit to widely different interpretations.

The key to real understanding is viewpoint. Every student of Nostradamus must hold continually in mind that the quatrains are the work of a medieval doctor with all the bigotry, intolerance and superstition of his age – a man ill-equipped to make sense of modern technology, morals or mores. At the same time, he was a keen observer and often recorded visions about which he may not have had the least understanding himself.

This said, we can do no better now than to plunge straight in and examine the world of our future, as seen through the eyes of the prophet of Salon more than four centuries ago. It will prove an exciting journey.

## First Century

The first fourteen quatrains of this Century are either occult or historical. The fifteenth is usually taken to refer to Napoleon, although Cheetham suggests very reasonably that it could equally well refer to the rise of the mullahs in Ayatollah Khomeini's Iran. The sixteenth quatrain reads:

**Quatrain 16**
Saturn and a water sign in Sagittarius
In its highest increase of exaltation
Pestilence, famine, death from military hand
The century approaches its renewal

The first two lines give an astrological indication of dating, but are insufficiently precise (there are three water signs) to be of any real use. If, however, it does relate to modern times, then no-one would argue with the description in line three. This is indeed an era of disease, famine and power too often seized at the barrel of a gun.

The final line is, however, particularly interesting in this context since Nostradamus speaks of 'renewal' as the century nears its close, suggesting rather better times ahead. This, for what it is worth, ties in with the ancient esoteric tradition of a dawning Age of Aquarius in which spiritual values would gradually take over from the old materialism. Depressing though the news may seem at times, our age must be viewed from the perspective of a dramatically increased awareness of ecological issues, spiritual values and even concern about human rights. Change is certainly slow – far too slow for many people – but it is definitely occurring on a far wider scale than ever before in human history.

**Quatrain 29**
When the fish of land and sea
By a great wave will be put on land
Its shape alien, smooth and horrible
By sea to the walls the enemies soon come

The description of an attack in the final line strongly suggests

that the 'fish' mentioned in the first is not a fish at all. Since
it can operate on land as well as at sea, Nostradamus may have
been watching an example of advanced technology in the form
of an amphibious craft, possibly even an amphibious submarine
which would, so far as I am aware, place it sometime in our own
future.

The smooth, threatening shape could, however, very easily
be a missile of some sort. Submarine crews have long referred
to torpedoes colloquially as 'fish'.

**Quatrain 46**
Close to Auch, Lectoure and Mirande
A great fire from heaven for three nights will fall
The cause will be seen as both amazing and miraculous
Afterwards the earth will tremble

This is the first of a number of quatrains in which, I believe,
Nostradamus may be predicting a visit to earth by beings from
another planet. This is such an outrageous suggestion that it
is as well to point out there is nothing inherently impossible
about it. While we can be sure that Earth is the only known
planet in our solar system to support intelligent life the
probability of life elsewhere in the universe is a statistical
certainty.

Given this, scientific objections to theories of extra-terrestrial
visitations are generally based on the enormous distances which
would have to be travelled, even from the nearest star. Since the
speed of light represents an absolute upper limit to the velocity
of any physical craft, inter-stellar journeys would have to be
measured in years – perhaps hundreds, even thousands of
years. What sort of being, the argument goes, would waste that
amount of time just to visit a backward planet of an obscure
solar system on the edge of a mediocre galaxy?

The answer, of course, is one that lives a great deal longer
than we do. [43]

If such a being were to visit our planet, the craft it used might well cause a 'great fire from heaven' for days and nights at a time. And without doubt the cause would be seen as both amazing and miraculous. The trembling of the earth may refer to the actual ship landing, or the reaction of the world population to the realization that humanity was no longer alone.

There is no indication of a date for this prediction, but other quatrains suggest such a landing may come about within the next decade and, as we shall see later, there have been certain scholarly and political developments which dramatically raise the probabilities in favour of its coming true.

### Quatrain 50
Under the aquatic triplicity will be born
One who will have Thursday for his holy day
His fame, praise, rule and power will increase
By land and sea to the troubled Orient

The Islamic holy day is Friday, the Jewish Saturday and the Christian Sunday. The adoption of Thursday as a new holy day suggests either the reform of an existing religion, or the appearance of a new one.

Nostradamus promises that, like the others, it will be founded by a male and will spread widely at a time when there is trouble in Asia and/or the Middle East. There are no clues to the dating of this development, but a study of ancient religions does suggest that reforms, or new revelations, arise fairly regularly and that we are currently overdue for the next. The first line of the prophecy tells us that Cancer, Scorpio and Pisces will be prominent in the horoscope of the founder.

### Quatrain 51
The leader of Aries, Jupiter and Saturn
God eternal, what changes
Then after a long century, the bad times will come again
France, Italy, what emotions

The next conjunction of Jupiter and Saturn in Aries is due, according to Erika Cheetham, on September 2, 1995 and she suggests the verse predicts a possible war beginning on that date. This seems a curious reading of the quatrain. What Nostradamus actually predicts is changes, which need not necessarily be for the worse. Indeed, when we consider the number of wars which have sparked across the globe since the beginning of the present century, it would seem far more reasonable to assume any change must herald a period of peace.

This interpretation is actually supported by the remainder of the quatrain for, following the changes, Nostradamus predicts a period of at least a hundred years before the 'bad times' come again. In such circumstances, the emotions of France and Italy are likely to be relief and joy.

### Quatrain 55
In a place with a climate opposite to that of Babylon
Great will be the bloodshed
Earth, sea, air and sky will be unequal
Sects, hunger, kingdoms, plagues, confusion

Since the climate of Babylon is hot, the 'place with an opposite climate' must be cold. Thus we are talking of some such territory as Iceland, Greenland, Lapland, Alaska, parts of China or Russia.

Wherever it is, Nostradamus predicts extensive bloodshed and the third line suggests this will come about through a natural disaster.[44] Hunger, illness and confusion are the usual aftermath of such catastrophes and fear often drives the population to take refuge in religion, hence the reference to sects. The addition of 'kingdoms' to the list is curious, but may signify a redrawing of national borders following the disaster.

### Quatrain 64
At night they will think to have seen the sun
When the pig, half human is seen

Noise, shouts, battles which appear fought in the sky
And brute beasts will be heard to speak

Erika Cheetham argues persuasively that this quatrain represents a medieval observer's attempt to make sense of an aerial battle in the twentieth century. Pilots wearing oxygen equipment do indeed present a pig-like snout in profile. She may, however, be on less solid ground when she interprets the final line as referring to radio communications – it is frankly difficult to see how Nostradamus could have perceived this as brute beasts talking. If, however, we link this prediction with Century 1, Quatrain 46, there is a small possibility that he was viewing the landing of a space vehicle. In this interpretation, the pilot would not, of course, be human and 'brute beasts heard to speak' becomes a primitive perception of extra-terrestrials.

## Quatrain 67

The great famine which I sense approaching
Will be often turned, then become universal
So vast and long lasting that you will seize
From woods the roots and the child from the breast

The words are clear enough and have a worrying contemporary ring to them. We have, over the past few decades, become accustomed to increasingly frequent appeals to subscribe to famine relief in Africa and Asia. Nostradamus foresees a time when such localized famines (which up to now we have been able to do something about) will eventually become world-wide and uncontrollable. Although such a prediction may have seemed extremely far-fetched even a single generation ago, only a very small shift in global climate would be needed to bring it about. Ecologists warn daily about the possibility of such a shift as a consequence of global warming or ozone layer depletion.

**Quatrain 87**
Earth-shaking fire from the centre of the earth
Will make tremble all around the new city
Two great rocks will make war for a long time
Then steam will redden a new river

The 'new city' is almost certainly New York. The quatrain clearly predicts a major earthquake and is especially interesting for its third line, which anticipates the theory of plate tectonics by centuries. The 'new river' may be a diversion of the Hudson, reddened by debris. Although the place is clearly pinpointed, there is no indication of the date.

**Quatrain 91**
The gods will make appearance to humans
That which they will be the authors of a great conflict
Before the sky was seen free of sword and lance
On the left hand the greatest damage will be inflicted

Our final quatrain from the first Century has been interpreted as predicting America's involvement in Vietnam or some similarly hi-tec war. Once again, however, the literal translation points us directly towards the theory of an extra-terrestrial visitation by aliens so advanced in their technology that they appear godlike.

If so, it seems that humanity will follow its old habit of striking first and asking questions afterwards for Nostradamus predicts a great conflict which will take place mainly in the sky. Sword and lance (which Cheetham translates as 'weapons and rockets') may be the closest the prophet could get to aerial missiles; and before the sky is free of them, one side will suffer far more damage than the other – a logical outcome since the visitors are likely to have far more advanced technology.

## Second Century

The first quatrain of the second Century points towards World War I. The second is usually taken to refer to Iran in the present era: although I find arguments supporting this position unconvincing, I can make no better suggestion of my own. The third quatrain, however, certainly seems to point to a situation which has not yet occurred . . . and which will not be particularly welcome when it does.

**Quatrain 3**
Because of the heat of the sun on the sea
Of Ruboea, the fish are half cooked
The locals will eat them
When in Rhodes and Genoa there will be little food

Erika Cheetham, who translates the opening line as 'Because of heat like that of the sun on the sea', suggests the verse refers to an atomic explosion somewhere in the Aegean. It is an intriguing idea, but I suspect a nuclear flash would burn the fish to a crisp, not merely half cook them.

If, as I believe, a better translation speaks of the heat of the sun itself and not something like it, then we may well be back to the disturbing effects of global warming. The fact that there is little food in Rhodes and Genoa may link this verse to Nostradamus' prediction of a global famine in Century 1, Quatrain 67, which we also speculated might arise due to environmental factors.

**Quatrain 8**
Temples made sacred in the first Roman fashion
They will reject the deep foundations
Taking their laws first and human
Throwing out not all the cults of saints

With his usual economy, Nostradamus shows that he is

speaking of the Roman Catholic Church while at the same time predicting a new religion (or a modification of the old one) based on pagan ('first Roman') principles. According to this description, the new development will not be linked with the old Roman gods, but will revive some of the early customs and legalities. Some familiar structures will remain, notably certain cults of the saints. Since there are clear prophecies elsewhere of the imminent demise of the Roman Church, this verse may describe either the cause or the result.

### Quatrain 13
The body without a soul is no longer put to the sacrifice
The day of death becomes the day of birth
The divine spirit will make the soul happy
Seeing the word in its eternity

Although one of his gentler prophecies, this could also be one of his most far-reaching. It predicts a time when reincarnation will be accepted as a tenet of the Christian religion. His Qabalistic studies show in his distinction (line 3) between spirit, the numinous essence of the individual, and soul, which is thought by occultists to be a subtle body associated with the emotions.

Taken as a whole, the verse speaks of an age when materialism no longer holds sway. In such an age, politicians can no longer impose death sentences based on the expediency of the here and now. With the acceptance of reincarnation as a Western religious tenet, an emotional need in the populace is fulfilled.

The last line is particularly interesting since to Catholic Nostradamus, the 'word' is likely to mean the Word of God, as revealed through the doctrines of the Church. The phrase 'seeing the word in its eternity' implies an historical totality. Perhaps not coincidentally, there is a school of thought which argues that reincarnation was a doctrine of early Christianity, later expunged from the canon for political ends.

**Quatrain 28**
The penultimate one to bear the prophet's name
Will take Monday for his day and rest
Travelling far in his frenzy
And delivering a great people from taxation

There are Islamic leaders to this day who claim descent from the Prophet Mohammet. It appears that the last but one of these will switch the Muslim holy day from Friday to Monday. The individual concerned seems fated to increase his power and may, like the Ayatollah Khomeini, actually manage to swallow up a whole nation. There may be a link here with Century 1, Quatrain 50, although the new holy day differs.

**Quatrain 41**
The great star through seven days will burn
So that two suns appear
The big mastiff all night howls
When the great pontiff changes his territory

The mention of 'two suns' suggests an unusually spectacular astronomical phenomenon – a comet or large meteor, perhaps, making a close approach to the earth. The appearance of the 'second sun' marks a change of residence for the current Pope and the howling of the guard-dog throughout the night is almost certainly an omen of death. The question then, is, to which Pope does the prophecy refer? According to Malachy, there will be only two more after John Paul II.

**Quatrain 62**
Mabus will soon come to die
Of people and animals a great destruction
Suddenly vengeance will be seen
One hundred, hand, thirst, hunger when passes the comet

'Mabus' is frequently put forward as the name of Nostradamus' third Antichrist and the quatrain as a whole taken to refer to the great destruction of the final war. If the comet is Halley's comet, however, the quatrain cannot be dated for 1999 to suit conventional millennial theory, but must be placed in 2062, the year the comet is next scheduled to enter solar orbit.

A second possibility arises however: Nostradamus may have watched in his visionary trance the Allied bombardment of Baghdad and mistaken the flight path of a missile for a comet. This certainly ties in with the idea of sudden vengeance. The war was mounted in response to the invasion of Kuwait and was characterized by fast punitive action. If this interpretation is correct, then the name 'Mabus' is another Nostradamus anagram, a reverse spelling made all the more obscure by the prophet having slightly misheard the name of the Iraqi leader (Sabum or Subam rather than Saddam).

The idea that Nostradamus may have witnessed Operation Desert Storm is further strengthened by our next quatrain.

**Quatrain 70**
The dart of heaven will make its journey
Death spoken of, great execution
The stone in the tree, the proud nation brought down
Rumour of a human monster, purge and expiation

The 'dart of heaven' is an even closer description of a missile as viewed from a medieval perspective. There was much talk of death before Desert Storm actually began – Saddam Hussein coined the colourful phrase 'Mother of Battles'. When the Allied attack finally began, it was executed as efficiently as any modern act of war and the 'proud nation' was brought down in double quick time. Saddam Hussein himself was frequently referred to as a 'human monster' although at the time of writing, his final purge and expiation is yet to take place.

**Quatrain 81**
By fire from the sky the city is almost razed
Flooding again threatens the Greek Noah
Sardinia vexed by the African fleet
After Libra leaves Leo

The final line seems to be an astrological dating which I am frankly unable to interpret, but the quatrain as a whole certainly points to a future war situation. There are similarities to the fate of Baghdad city, which was almost razed by fire from the sky during Desert Storm, but the remainder of the verse makes it clear that some other action is forecast at a time when there is extensive flooding in Greece. The African fleet which vexes Sardinia may represent a naval build-up by North African countries like Libya or Egypt, or, since political situations can change out of all recognition over the years, possibly even South Africa or one of the Black African states.

**Quatrain 95**
Populated lands will be uninhabitable
Over fields there will be great disagreement
Kingdoms given over to those incapable of prudence
Then the great brothers, Death and Dissension

Another quatrain frequently referred to as predicting the biblical 'last days' but rather more likely to foretell the changes that must inevitably follow global warming. As lands which formerly supported a reasonable population gradually turn to desert, there will be increasing disagreement over what shrinking areas of arable land are left. Inevitably leaders will come to power who are incapable of meeting the crisis, with widespread death and dissension following.

# Third Century

### Quatrain 40
The great theatre will again be built
Dice thrown and nets cast
The leader who sounds the knell grows tired
By bows destroyed a long time made

As Erika Cheetham remarks, the line about the dice and nets is reminiscent of the Roman Games, although she finds the remainder of the verse obscure. In fact it seems to predict a time in which cultural values have changed sufficiently to permit a revival of the Games in a rebuilt Coliseum – or at least something very like them. The verse also contains a prediction of a political assassination using bows, possibly because the individual in question had hi-tec protection against more modern weapons.

### Quatrain 60
In the whole of Asia there will be a great proscription
The same in Mysia, Lycia and Pamphilia
Blood shed because of absolution
Of a young leader filled with evil deeds

Absolution is a term suggesting reprieve, amnesty or even forgiveness. This quatrain points to a time when the world will have cause to regret that it did not completely put down an evil leader. Asia may in this instance mean Asia Minor, since the names mentioned in the second line are all of countries which once existed in the Middle East – Lycia, for example, stretched across what is now the Anatolia province of Turkey. It seems fairly likely then, that the quatrain as a whole refers to the plight of the Kurds in the days following cessation of hostilities in the Gulf War when the Allies made the decision to halt before Saddam Hussein was toppled.

**Quatrain 92**
The world close to the last days
Saturn will again be slow to return
The empire moves towards the Brodde nation
The eye plucked from Narbonne by a goshawk

Here, for the first time, we have an unmistakable reference to the 'last days' – but not, as so many commentators would have us believe, in the year 2000. To reconcile this quatrain with the remainder of Nostradamus' prophecies, we need to postulate a date at least five thousand years later. Narbonne, an ancient city in southeastern France, still survives, but I can find no reference in any of my encyclopaedias to the 'Brodde nation'. Any empire which has arisen five thousand years from now must be equally incomprehensible. Unless Nostradamus is right about reincarnation, it is unlikely that any of today's readers will be in a position to check out the truth of this prophecy.

**Quatrain 97**
New law to occupy new land
Around Syria, Judea and Palestine
The great non-Christian empire will crumble
Before the twentieth century is done

As many other commentators have pointed out, this is a classic quatrain describing the establishment of the modern state of Israel on May 14, 1948. Since then, there have been four major Arab-Israeli wars (1947-9, 1956, 1967, and 1973) and numerous intermittent battles. Although Egypt and Israel signed a peace treaty in 1979, hostility between Israel and the rest of its Arab neighbours, complicated by the demands of Palestinian Arabs, has continued up to the time of writing. Nostradamus predicts, however, that the great Arab alliance against Israel will crumble before the end of the present century – a real possibility given increasing dissension among the Arab nations.

## Fourth Century

The fourth Century begins with the usual mixture of wars, calamities and the fate of kings. Then comes one of the most peculiar quatrains Nostradamus ever wrote, reflecting the bewilderment of the prophet himself as he penned it:

Quatrain 24
Where the faint voice of woman is heard beneath sacred ground
A human flame shines with the divine voice
The celibates with their blood will stain the earth
And the holy temples destroyed for the impure ones

The verse has puzzled commentators, who occasionally refer it to the persecution of the clergy during the French Revolution. In fact it seems far more likely to be a somewhat male chauvinistic viewpoint on the controversy surrounding the admission of women to the Christian priesthood.

Although it is difficult to maintain that the female voice is in any sense less divine than the male, the existing (male) priesthood metaphorically bleeds at the thought of their temples being, as they see it, desecrated by the 'impure' daughters of Eve.

Quatrain 32
In places and times where meat gives way to fish
The law of the land will be turned around
The old will hold strong, then be removed from the scene
All things held in common put behind

The doctrine of all things held in common is, of course, Communism and this quatrain gives a vivid description of the breakdown of the Communist structures of Eastern Europe, a process that continues at the time of writing. Nostradamus correctly states that the trouble started over food – the first real cracks in the monolith appeared when there were strikes about the price of food in Poland. The law of the land was turned around when the illegal trade union, Solidarity, was formed. The old guard at first held strong when martial law was proclaimed, but were later removed altogether. Interestingly, Nostradamus clearly predicts in the final line that all traces of Communism will eventually disappear from the world.

### Quatrain 43

There will be heard in the sky weapons battling
During a year when religious people are enemies
They will wish the holy laws unjustly to be discussed
By lightning and war good believers are put to death

Aerial warfare is obviously forecast in this quatrain, although as often happens with Nostradamus, there is no particular indication of when it may break out. The prophet does hint that the cause of the war will be religious, possibly pointing towards yet another Arab-Israeli conflict in the Middle East or renewed fighting between India and Pakistan. There is even a small chance it may refer to Northern Ireland where there have been occasional terrorist rocket attacks on British Army helicopters. The final line contains more than a hint of irony: it is the good believers who die in this war about right faith.

### Quatrain 95

The rule of two will be held only a little while
Three years seven months pass, then there will be war
The two vassals rebel against them
The winner born on American soil

The fashionable explanation that this quatrain forecasts the breakdown of US – Soviet detente is somewhat unsatisfactory, if only because it seems already to have held up more than three years and seven months. And where do we find even one vassal state of both superpowers simultaneously, let alone two?

A more plausible explanation may be drawn from the first line which hints at some sort of joint leadership of a country. The most likely candidate at present is the Soviet Union where it is becoming increasingly obvious that Premier Gorbachev will not be able to maintain his hold on power without some sort of deal with Russian President Boris Yeltzin. This could quite easily develop into a joint leadership agreement, but if so, Nostradamus predicts it will break up again in just over three years, following rebellion by two of the vassal states, possibly the Baltic Republics. And the winner of such a rebellion would, of course, be America which even in the post-Cold War period stands to gain from a weakened USSR.

**Quatrain 99**
The valiant eldest son of the daughter of a King
Repulses the French profoundly
Using thunderbolts, how many in such numbers
Few and distant, then deeply into the Western lands

While the prediction speaks specifically of a battle against the French,[45] there are elements in this quatrain which suggest the use or threat of intercontinental ballistic missiles capable of penetrating well beyond French borders. This plainly places it in the modern era, although there is no way of telling how far in the future it should be placed.


# Fifth Century

There are no obvious modern-day predictions in the fifth Century until the eighth quatrain, in which Nostradamus again returns to hi-tec warfare.

**Quatrain 8**
There will be loosed living fire and hidden death
Within spheres horrible and frightening

At night by the fleet a city will be reduced to rubble
The city on fire, the enemy favourable

The verse might describe the atomic bombing of Hiroshima or Nagasaki already discussed were it not for the mention of a fleet. Certainly fire and death hidden in spheres is strongly suggestive of bombs. We may be reading of an event yet to come, but the quatrain fits very closely the fate of Baghdad which suffered intense aerial bombardment, mainly at night, from planes carried by the American fleet. An even earlier possibility would be the coastal bombardment of Beirut by American warships during the Reagan presidency.

**Quatrain 25**
The warlike Arab prince, sun, Venus, Lyons
Rule of the church by the sea shall fall
Towards Iran almost a million men
Byzantium, Egypt ver.serp. invade

During the Iran-Iraq War, when the Ayatollah Khomeini was believed (in the West) to be the world's greatest villain, this quatrain was generally thought to forecast an Iranian push through Egypt and Turkey, sparking World War Three and the nuclear Armageddon. It did not happen. With the Ayatollah dead, a calmer reading may take note of the fact that the million men are seen moving towards Iran, not out of it. This may suggest an Iraqi attack, except that the numbers involved do not seem nearly enough to mount a successful invasion of Egypt and Turkey in the immediate future, given that both would certainly receive the same sort of Western support as Kuwait.

This then throws us back to the possibility that the prediction refers to a more distant future when, perhaps due to the discovery of a cheap substitute for oil, the industrialized countries have abandoned their interest in the Middle East. The term 'ver.serp.' in the final line remains mysterious, incidentally. Cheetham thinks it may be a Latin abbreviation and translates it as 'true serpent'.

**Quatrain 27**
By fire and arms not far from the Black Sea
He will come from Iran to take Trebizond
Pharos and Mytilene tremble
With Arab blood the Adriatic is covered

Trebizond is a Black Sea port in northeastern Turkey, so that this quatrain may enlarge on the situation described in the last prediction we examined, although in this verse the villain clearly does come from Iran. Perhaps Nostradamus was attempting to describe the sort of confusion that frequently arises in widespread warfare, in which one country, then another may invade a third. If so, he clearly suggests in the final line that the Arabs as a whole will bear the brunt of the suffering.

**Quatrain 68**
In the Danube and from the Rhine will come to drink
The great Camel who will not repent
Those of the Rhone tremble, those of the Loire even more so
And near the Alps the cock will ruin him

The theme of Islamic expansion is again taken up, this time with a deep push into Europe. Mention of the Danube suggests Austria, Hungary, Yugoslavia, and Romania through which it flows. The Rhine could signify Switzerland, Germany, or the Netherlands. No wonder there is consternation, but Nostradamus forecasts that the French (symbolized by the cock) will stop the enemy in his tracks during a battle near the Alps.

**Quatrain 73**
Persecuted will be the church of God
And the holy churches will be despoiled
The child of the mother will be put naked in a chemise
The Arabs will make alliance with the Poles

To Nostradamus, the 'church of God' could only be the Roman Catholic church. The 'child of the mother' is most likely to be the infant Jesus, cast down as churches are despoiled in some future persecution. There is a clear suggestion in the final line that the persecution may be at the hands of Islam, but since today's Poland is a staunchly Catholic country, any alliance would seem unlikely in the immediate future.

**Quatrain 78**
The two will not hold together for long
And in thirteen years to barbarian power
On both sides there will be so much loss
That the Barque and its Captain will be blessed

This verse is reminiscent of Century 4, Quatrain 95 and some commentators have claimed it refers to the same situation, despite the discrepancy in the time during which the two are predicted to hold together (thirteen years here, three years and seven months in the earlier quatrain). If so, we may yet be treated to the surprising spectacle of two Russian leaders thanking the Vatican and its Pope – symbolically referred to in the final line – for help in sorting out their differences.

**Quatrain 81**
The royal bird on the city of the sun
Seven months before there will be nightly omens
The Wall of the East will fall, thunder, lightning
Seven days to the gates the enemies come

While it is difficult to make much of the first line of this quatrain, the remainder is clear enough. For months before the event itself, there were clear signs that huge changes were underway in Eastern Europe. Then came the most dramatic development of all, the fall of the Berlin wall, a symbol of division since 1961. As Nostradamus foresaw, former enemies crowded the old gates and checkpoints to stream into West Berlin.

**Quatrain 90**
In the Cyclades, Perinthus and Larissa
Within Sparta all of the Peloponesus
So great a famine caused by pestilence
Nine months it will hold throughout the land

Currently we think of famine in association with Africa or Asia, but in this quatrain, Nostradamus predicts famine throughout Greece – and a long-lasting famine at that. The most interesting aspect of the verse is the suggestion that the famine is caused by disease. This is a theme to which Nostradamus returns, as we shall see.

**Quatrain 98**
On the 48th degree of the climacteric
At the end of Cancer so great a drought
Fish in the sea, river, lake furiously boiled
Berne and Bigorre by fire from heaven distressed

The geographical reference in the first line places this quatrain in France. The astrological reference in the second states the event will take place in summer, probably the month of July. If this prediction refers back to Quatrain 68, then the 'fire from heaven' probably refers to military bombardment. If not, Nostradamus may have been speaking of violent lightning storms. The reference to sea, river and lake waters boiling sounds suspiciously like a nuclear or laser attack, since even the most pessimistic scientists stop short of claiming the greenhouse effect will run sufficiently riot to boil water.

## Sixth Century

The sixth Century opens with a quatrain that could possibly be futuristic, although this is not definite. This is followed by three that are almost certainly historical. Then comes a sobering verse that has all the hallmarks of a prediction for our immediate future.

### Quatrain 5
So great a famine from a wave of pestilence
That rains a long time the length of the Arctic Pole
Samarobrin is a hundred leagues from the hemisphere
They will live without law, exempt from politics

Famine, like the poor, is always with us, but in this quatrain, Nostradamus suggests it arises from a long-lasting plague so widespread that it actually reaches the polar regions. I am not the first to suggest this plague could be AIDS, or Acquired Immune Deficiency Syndrome, which was first reported at Bellevue-New York University Medical Centre in 1979 and has since become an international epidemic. Erika Cheetham makes the ingenious but persuasive suggestion that 'Samarobrin' might be a curative drug[46] manufactured on a satellite or orbiting space station ('a hundred leagues from the hemisphere'). The final line of the prophecy is especially chilling since it pictures AIDS victims as living in isolation, like lepers.

### Quatrain
When those of the North Pole are assembled
In the East will be great fear and trembling
A new man elected, sustaining a great shivering
Rhodes, Byzantium stained by un-Christian blood

Although this quatrain is frequently given an apocalyptic interpretation involving East-West war, the reference to the North Pole suggests a link with the quatrain we have just examined. If so, then the idea of quarantine for AIDS victims is taken a step further with the idea of an isolation colony somewhere in the polar regions.

At a time when this colony has been established, the

prophecy implies, the epidemic has a firm hold throughout Asia and the West, so that even a world leader may be infected. The phrase 'stained by un-Christian blood' is particularly apposite, given the religious-based viewpoint Nostradamus would have been likely to adopt towards a venereal disease. Even in our supposedly more enlightened age, there are fundamentalists who insist AIDS is a visitation by God on account of human sin. Nostradamus could easily have considered infected blood 'un-Christian'.

### Quatrain 34
The fiery flying machine
Will come to bring trouble to the great chief
Within it there will be such sedition
That those abandoned will be in despair

Although the meaning of this verse is clear enough, there is insufficient detail to place it in any particular country or time. I have included it largely because of the exceptionally straightforward opening line, which marks it out at once as a modern quatrain. While it may yet prove to be a prediction of our future, it is worth considering the possibility that Nostradamus was watching the Hindenburg, a rigid airship built in Germany in 1936, which became the world's first transatlantic commercial airliner. While manoeuvring to land at Lakehurst on May 6, 1937, the airship's hydrogen ignited and the Hindenburg was destroyed by the resulting fire. Thirty-five passengers and crew died, along with one member of the ground crew. Claims that the Hindenburg was a victim of sabotage have never been supported by evidence, but the third line of the Nostradamus quatrain would suggest they had some substance.

### Quatrain 66
On the establishment of the new sect
There will be found the bones of a great Roman

A marble sepulchre will be uncovered
The earth will tremble in April, badly buried

The 'great Roman' is often taken to be St Peter, a theory
supported by the religious associations of the first line, but the
possibility that the find involves the remains of a Caesar,
Senator or General should not be ruled out. Although no hint
of the year is given, we should watch out for the news in April,
with the discovery probably resulting from the partial
disclosure of the tomb as the result of an earthquake.

### Century 6, Quatrain 74
She who was dismissed will return to reign
Her enemies found in the conspirators
More than ever will her time be triumphant
Seventy-three to death most certainly

This quatrain is generally accredited to Elizabeth I of England
despite the fact that she died at the age of seventy and not, as
the verse states, seventy-three. I believe a rather better
candidate would be Benazir Bhutto, who made history when
she became Pakistan's first woman Prime Minister, but was
subsequently removed from office by Presidential decree. If my
interpretation of Nostradamus is correct, we may yet see her
returned to power with the promise of living to a ripe old age.

### Quatrain 97
Forty-five degrees the sky will be alight
Fire approaches the great new city
At once a great flame springs up
When they wish to see the Normans proven

Apocalyptic interpreters view this verse as predicting nuclear
attack on New York, but there are at least twenty-five other
place-names beginning with the word 'new' and the reference
to the Normans would suggest Nostradamus was actually

viewing an incident in France, not America. The most likely possibility is a widespread fire, reflected in the night sky. Once again, no hint of a year is given.

## Seventh Century

This truncated Century – it has only forty-two quatrains in all – does not seem to contain predictions of particular relevance to our own future.

## Eighth Century

The second verse of this Century has elements which may just mark it out as belonging to the twentieth century or later.

### Quatrain 2
At Condom and Aux and around Mirande
I see coming from the sky fire which envelops them
The sun and Mars conjoined in Leo then Marmande
Lightning, great hail and a wall collapses in Garonne

A term like 'fire from the sky' always carries the possibility of aerial bombardment, but in the final line the reference to lightning suggests a natural phenomenon at a time of very severe weather. The mention of Garonne sets the prediction either in France or Spain. The Garonne river rises in the Pyrenees and flows northeast through Spain then northwest through southwest France. It reaches the Atlantic Ocean a short distance north of Bordeaux.

### Quatrain 9
While the eagle and cock are at Savona
There will be united the Levantine Sea and Hungary
The army to Naples, Palermo, the marches of Ancona
Rome, Venice, a horrible cry by the dart

The Eagle and the Cock are, respectively, America and France. While the remainder of the quatrain is difficult, it seems to describe a time when, during a great power conference, there will be an alliance formed between Hungary and an eastern maritime power. The rest of the verse suggests war, or at least military mobilization, in Italy, with the term 'dart' a possible reference to a missile.

### Quatrain 21

To the port of Agde three foists will enter
Carrying the infection of the pestilence, not the faith
Passing the bridge, a thousand thousand will be taken
And the bridge broken by the resistance of a third one

Ship-borne plague might suggest an historical quatrain and even the numbers involved do not, as Erika Cheetham suggests, absolutely place it in the twentieth century. All the same, it is tempting to link this verse with others we have studied and see it as yet another prediction of the effects of the AIDS epidemic.

### Quatrain 62

When the sacred temples are seen plundered
The greatest of the lands profaning sacred things
Because of their actions an enormous pestilence will arrive
The king will not condemn them for the injustice

The twentieth century has seen profound cultural changes, not least of them a dramatic slackening of the grip of orthodox religion on the public mind. Nostradamus would certainly have viewed this as a time when sacred temples were plundered and the greatest of the land profaned sacred things. Like every educated doctor of his age, he firmly believed that plague was a judgment of God, so it is no surprise to find his linking profanity and pestilence as cause and effect. If we have the timing right on this one, the pestilence almost certainly has to be AIDS. Interestingly, Nostradamus shows in the final line that modern viewpoint does not generally make the same connection between God's will and disease as he does.

### Quatrain 70
He enters the picture, wicked, unpleasant, infamous
Tyrannizing Mesopotamia
All friends are made by the adulterous woman
Land horrible, black of face

This is arguably the clearest, most concise biography it would be possible to write on the Iraqi leader, Saddam Hussein. Although the effective ruler of Iraq from 1976, and instigator of the Iran-Iraq War in September 1980, he really only attracted the attention of the world Press on his annexation of Kuwait. He entered the picture, exactly as Nostradamus predicted, wicked, unpleasant and infamous. Commentator after commentator suddenly discovered his responsibility for such atrocities as chemical attacks on Kurdish villages.

In modern usage the term Mesopotamia refers to most of what is now Iraq and it soon became clear that Saddam Hussein terrorized his own country just as much as his neighbours. I suspect the 'adulterous woman' in the third line is actually a biblical reference – Nostradamus may be likening him to the notorious Whore of Babylon, particularly apt since the ancient capital of southern Mesopotamia was situated only about 90 km (55 miles) south of modern Baghdad. The final line refers to the situation in Iraq following Operation Desert Storm.

### Quatrain 77
The Antichrist quickly annihilates three
Twenty-seven years of blood will last his war
The heretics dead, captive or exiled
Bloody corpses, water red, covering the earth

One of the very rare direct uses of the term 'Antichrist' in the quatrains. (Many commentators – myself included – have sought to identify the three Antichrists which Nostradamus discusses elsewhere, but the prophet himself uses the actual term only twice in the quatrains so far as I can discover; and on neither occasion linked to a name.)

In the present verse, twenty-seven years of bloody religious war are promised, following the annihilation of three countries (or possibly hostages). There is, however, no indication of dating.

### Quatrain 99
By the power of three temporal kings
To another place will the sacred throne be moved
Where the substance of the spirit body
Will be put back and received by the true throne

The sacred throne, which to Nostradamus could only mean the Papacy, was moved from Rome once before and, according to this prophecy, will be moved again, for political rather than religious reasons. (Italian denunciation of the Concordat with the Vatican State would be sufficient to provoke such a move.) All the same, Nostradamus foresees some good coming out of it, since it appears to renew the spirit and vigour of the Church.

## Ninth Century

The early quatrains of the ninth Century refer to such interesting phenomena as two-headed monsters, but it is not until we are almost a third of the way through that we reach this fascinating, surprising and, above all, disturbing, quatrain:

### Quatrain 31
The ground trembles at Mortara
Cornwall of St George half sunk
By peace made drowsy, war erupts
In the church at Easter, abyss opens

This verse is frightening enough in the version I have given, but the term I have translated as 'Cornwall' is literally rendered 'tin island' and might therefore refer to the whole of Britain. Either way, there seems to be a very difficult time coming with huge tracts of British soil sinking beneath the sea in an earthquake. Then, when everybody least expects it, the country plunges into war. The timing is Easter, but the dating is not given.

Some commentators decline to accept that the 'tin island of St George' could be Britain since it lies distant from the world's main earthquake zones. Despite this, however, there was a major earthquake – fortunately with minimal damage – which affected the whole of the British Isles just a few years ago from the time of writing. Its epicentre was just off the Welsh coast.

The mention of Mortara, however, suggests the quake will be far more massive and widespread than anything ever before experienced in this part of the world. Mortara is a town in Italy, roughly midway between Torino and Milano. If, as Nostradamus suggests, the epicentre of the quake lies there, then it would have to be a quake of quite extraordinary violence to influence the British Isles, let alone sink a goodly portion of them. There is, however, the possibility that 'Mortara' is an anagram for a British placename, although if so, I have been unable to crack it.

### Quatrain 55
The horrible war which the West prepared
The year following will come the pestilence
So greatly horrible that neither young, old nor beast
Blood, fire, Mercury, Mars, Jupiter in France

In this quatrain, Nostradamus times the most dramatic spread of AIDS in relation to a 'horrible war' prepared by the West. One wonders if the war referred to might be Operation Desert Storm which, though limited in its objectives, shocked many observers by its sheer ferocity. If so, then we do not have long to wait for the epidemic.

## Tenth Century

In the early quatrains of this final Century we read of such historical occurrences as the Battle of Worcester and, as we have already seen, the abdication of Edward VIII. Then comes a quatrain which may, on the one hand, be wholly unimportant . . . or it may, on the other hand, provide us with a vital clue to some of Nostradamus' most dramatic prophecies.

### Quatrain 32
The Empire each year should grow great
One will come to power over the others
But only a short time will endure his kingdom and life
Two years will he be able to sustain himself by his ships

In my analysis of earlier quatrains, I suggested Nostradamus foresaw visits by extra-terrestrials in humanity's future and tried to show that, however outlandish the idea might appear, it is by no means utterly impossible. The present quatrain raises a new, different and highly intriguing possibility. If one came across the verse out of context, there is no doubt at all that it reads like a publicity synopsis for George Lucas' Star Wars series of movies. Could we take seriously the proposition that this might be exactly what it was? We know almost nothing of the mechanics of prophecy beyond the fact that Nostradamus used ritual techniques to place himself in trance. We have no idea how he 'viewed' future events or what, if any criteria, he used to separate fact from fiction. Is it possible that a man from medieval France, accidentally 'tuning in' to a twentieth-century movie theatre, might mistake the dramatic and bewildering screen images for reality? If Nostradamus somehow 'watched' Star Wars or, perhaps, other science fiction epics, it would make sense of some of his most bizarre and apocalyptic predictions.

**Quatrain 49**
The world garden near the new city
In the road of the hollow mountains
It will be seized and plunged in the tank
Made by force to drink water made poisonous by sulphur

With a remarkable, but very reasonable, leap of imagination, Erika Cheetham wonders if the 'road of the hollow mountains' might be a street in New York City, the 'hollow mountains' being the best description Nostradamus could coin for skyscrapers. The remainder of the quatrain describes the poisoning of the city's water supply, with the strong suggestion that this comes about through a deliberate act. If so, this could be a description of a terrorist outrage.

**Quatrain 66**
The chief of London by foreign [l'Americh] power
The isle of Scotland burdened by ice
Rob Roy will have so dreadful an Antichrist
Who gets everyone into trouble

The second quatrain with a specific mention of an Antichrist, but one that presents considerable difficulties in interpretation. The more usual translation of 'l'Americh' is 'American' not 'foreign' but this makes little sense of the reference to Rob Roy in line three.[47]

Rob Roy was Robert MacGregor, a Highland freebooter known as the Scottish Robin Hood, who lived from 1671 to 1734. Nominally a cattle dealer, he became a cattle thief who sold his neighbours protection against other rustlers. When the protection business failed, he was declared an outlaw and warred with his principal creditor the Duke of Montrose until 1722, when he was forced to surrender. Later imprisoned, he was finally pardoned in 1727. If my interpretation is correct, this is not, of course, a futuristic quatrain, but I have included it in the overall analysis as indicative of the loose way in which

Nostradamus may have used the term 'Antichrist' – much as
the modern usage, 'The devil got into him.'

### Quatrain 71
The land and air will freeze so much water
When they come to venerate Thursday
He who comes will never be so fair
Of the four quarters that honour him

This quatrain obviously refers back to Quatrain 50 of Century
1 which speaks of the adoption of Thursday as a holy day. The
importance of the present verse is the first line which suggests
that at the time this comes about, the world might be moving
into a new Ice Age.

### Quatrain 72
The year 1999 and seven months
From the sky will come a great King of Terror
Resuscitating the great King of the Mongols
Before which Mars reigns happily

There is a certain irony in the fact that our examination of
Nostradamus' prophecies ends with his most specific and
apocalyptic. The marvellously dramatic imagery of the 'King
of Terror', the terminal reference to the god of war, and the
precise dating – only eight years away as I write – have all
combined to send chills down the spines of modern readers and
even inspired a somewhat inaccurate movie on Nostradamus
starring Orson Welles.[48] Almost without exception,
commentators have taken it as predicting the end of the world,
although there is nothing in the verse to indicate this is what
Nostradamus really meant.

The final line of the quatrain tells of a period before 1999 in
which Mars reigns happily – an accurate enough description of
the current age, but one which also suggests the reign of Mars
might actually come to an end in 1999. This is not so outlandish

as it appears, since there is a long tradition of warring factions burying their differences in the face of a common threat. The threat itself is, of course, embodied in the King of Terror.

Conventional wisdom has the King of Terror as a national leader – the Welles movie, drawing together a number of quatrains, portrays him as a devilishly handsome Arab in a blue turban – but the verse itself specifically states he comes 'from the sky' and not from any particular country. In the following line, we see him capable of miracles since he revives the great King of the Mongols, dead since 1227,[49] although it may be that the resuscitation is not to be taken literally.

In the circumstances, it is reasonable to ask whether the King of Terror is a man at all, let alone the Antichrist so often claimed. Taken in conjunction with other quatrains of the same ilk, is it possible we are back to the extra-terrestrial hypothesis, with national and international differences abruptly dwarfed by the appearance of a terrifying, but technically advanced, alien life form capable of cloning the cells of our ancient dead to produce a spurious resurrection?

Incredibly, there is a growing body of evidence to suggest this hypothesis is beginning to find favour among the most pragmatic and hard-headed of our modern world leaders.

The first indication of the trend arose with SETI, the Search for Extra Terrestrial Intelligence Institute in California. This organisation, staffed by high-powered scientists, established a number of projects in an attempt to monitor radio emissions in space for indications of intelligent signals. For years, a cynical US Congress systematically reduced funds for these projects and, in 1982, cut them off altogether. The following year, 1983, the policy was abruptly reversed. SETI was funded once again.

1983 was the year President Reagan announced his Strategic Defence ('Star Wars') Initiative. The projected laser shield was widely taken to be a defence against attack by the Soviet Union. Up to this time, Reagan had condemned the Soviets as an 'Evil Empire', introduced cruise missiles into Europe, launched a massive rearmament programme and refused to renew the 1972 space cooperation agreement. Despite all this, the US President insisted the USSR had nothing to fear from the proposed new initiative.

The Soviets did not believe him. Mikhail Gorbachev swept to power in 1985 insisting that any improvement in Soviet – US relations depended absolutely on the abandonment of Star Wars. But only months later, everything had changed.

The Press first noted the shift in the attitude of Soviet space scientists. After years of near-paranoid secrecy, there was a new openness – despite the plain fact that the Soviets were substantially ahead in the space race at that time and consequently had little to gain by sharing information. One result of the new attitude was the possibility of cooperation in a programme to explore Mars. With Star Wars still firmly in place, the old space cooperation agreement was suddenly renewed. Soviet space officials travelled to Washington, American Congressmen visited Russian space facilities.

In November 1985, the first Gorbachev – Reagan summit was held. Political observers gave small odds for its success, yet the superpower leaders emerged proclaiming a new era of trust and understanding. How had it come about? In his first public appearance after the summit, President Reagan claimed he told First Secretary Gorbachev, 'Just think how easy his task and mine might be in these meetings that we held if suddenly there was a threat to this world from some other species from another planet outside this universe.'

President Reagan returned to the theme of extra terrestrials in March the following year when he met a group of space scientists and asked them if they had any evidence of other peoples 'out there'. On being told they had not, he remarked that he hoped they would have 'more excitement' as time went on.

It was beginning to sound as though the President was rehearsing the script of one of his old B-movies, but then in 1987, President Gorbachev suddenly joined in. He revealed to a Kremlin forum that he and President Reagan had discussed the possibility of the US and the USSR joining forces to repel an invasion from outer space. Gorbachev went on to make light of the possibility, but added that he 'would not dispute the hypothesis'.

Behind the scenes, the hypothesis was not being disputed either. An international working committee was set up in the US to determine official attitudes towards any detection of extra-terrestrial intelligence – and, in particular, how much, if anything, the public should be told about such a discovery.

As a joint US–USSR Mars programme moved from theory into the reality of a new cooperation agreement, President Reagan told the General Assembly of the United Nations on 21 September 1987, 'Perhaps we [humanity] need some outside universal threat to recognize our common bond. I occasionally think how quickly our differences would vanish if we were facing an alien threat from outside the world'.

He made it sound hypothetical, but only sixteen days earlier, Reagan had bluntly asked Soviet Foreign Minister Eduard Shevardnadze to confirm that the USSR would join the US in defence of the planet against a threat from outer space. Shevardnadze replied, 'Yes, absolutely'.

In May 1988, President Reagan remarked soberly to the National Strategy Forum, 'What would happen if all of us in the world discovered that we were threatened by . . . a power from outer space, from another planet?'

The Working Committee on official attitudes answered that question in a paper published the following year. Among the guidelines set for handling the discovery of any intelligent signal from an extra-terrestrial source, they included that the information should be kept secret and no reply should be sent before international consultation.

Meanwhile, SETI funding was doubled, then tripled. It looked as though those in authority had begun to take ET very seriously indeed.

One man who thinks he knows why is Zecharia Sitchin, the author of a series of books called *The Earth Chronicles*. Sitchin believes, with a majority of astronomers, that there is an additional undiscovered planet in our solar system. Among astro-physicists, this belief is based on perturbations in the orbits of the outer planets and of Halley's comet. Sitchin, however, bases his conclusions not on modern findings, but on ancient documents – mainly Sumerian – which have led him to the theory that the 'missing planet' follows a cometary orbit bringing it close to Earth every 3,600 years.

But Sitchin does not stop there. He is convinced – on the basis of an impressive array of evidence – that the missing planet is inhabited by intelligent beings who have visited Earth in the past and may well do so again when their world comes close enough. [50] Is it this visit which Nostradamus forecasts for 1999? The timing is about right and, chillingly, the *Washington Post* reported in 1984:

> A heavenly body . . . possibly part of this solar system has been found in the direction of the constellation Orion by an orbiting telescope . . . When . . . scientists first saw the mystery object . . . there was some speculation that it might be moving toward Earth . . .

It is odd to think that a journey which began in a little attic room in medieval France may have led us to the threatening depths of outer space, yet any study of Nostradamus has to be conducted with a totally open mind. There is no doubt at all that Michel de Nostredame could predict the future. Despite claims that his prophecies are too generalised and obscure to have any evidential value, it is clear from his quatrains that he was capable of naming dates, names and quite specific circumstances, even though he did not always choose to do so.

His writings show he was frequently appalled by what he saw – the French Revolution and its aftermath were as alien to him as any extra-terrestrial contact would be to us – but, as he told his son César, he felt morally obliged to face the facts of his visions. In attempting to interpret them one step removed, we can do no better than to try to follow his example.

# Notes

1 There is strong evidence that our robed man was familiar with the first two named works, since he quoted from them in his writings. Historian James Laver suggests he must also have known the latter which was – and still is – one of the most popular magical grimoires of all time.

2 The historians in question are, respectively, Ward and Laver. One suspects each placed his own interpretation on a record of '12 o'clock'.

3 And apparently believed it all. In later years he dosed the Bishop of Carcassonne with a compound of lapiz lazuli, coral and gold leaf which, he claimed, included amongst less important properties the ability to 'augment the sperm in such abundance that a man can do whatever he wishes without damaging his health'.

4 John Hogue in his *Nostradamus and the Millennium*, Bloomsbury Publishing, London, 1987.

5 I am indebted to George Wilson who points out that lignum aloes would have had a magical as well as herbal use in Nostradamus' mind. The wood is an ingredient in many ritual incenses and perfumes, notably those dedicated to the Sun and Jupiter.

6 It was jokingly reported afterwards that Mrs Meir offered to fight the Vietnam War for US President Lyndon Johnson at cost plus 10%.

7 The boy was actually only a few weeks old at the time.

8   Or perhaps not as impressive as all that since his journey to the Court had cost him at least 100 écus of his own money. There were, however, subsequent and generous indications of royal favour.

9   The haughty Philip II could not be persuaded to travel to Paris even to claim a bride.

10   In *The Prophecies of Nostradamus*, Corgi Books, London, 1989.

11   This sort of reasoning is not nearly so strained as it looks. Nostradamus filled his prophecies with just such convoluted codings.

12   One of her astrologers, the roguish Cosmo Ruggieri, had long before warned her to 'beware of St Germain'. Curiously, the priest who administered the last rites was called Julien de St Germain.

13   Difficult, but not quite impossible. *The Jupiter Effect*, by John Gribbin and Stephen Plagemann (Fontana/Collins, London, 1977) argues the possibility that Jupiter's gravitational field may be among the factors involved in earthquakes. This is, however, a far cry from traditional astrology which looks on Jupiter, by and large, as the harbinger of good fortune.

14   Quoted from *Cosmic Influences on Human Behaviour* by Michel Gauquelin, Aurora Press, New York, 1985.

15   Quoted from *The Cosmic Clocks* by Michel Gauquelin, Paladin Books, St Albans, 1973.

16   While not exactly commonplace, such visionary 'windows' are not all that rare either. I have experienced the phenomenon twice myself: once at a spiritualist séance and once during experiments in reincarnation research.

17   Specifically *Nostradamus and the Millennium*.

18   John Hogue.

19   In *The Prophecies of Nostradamus*.

20   A disc, made from wood or metal, inscribed on both sides and used for the control of spirits.

21   A contemporary of Christ, Apollonius was a Pythagorean

initiate believed to exercise miraculous powers.

22   In *The Prophecies of Nostradamus.*

23   In *Nostradamus: the Future Foretold*, George Mann, 1973.

24   Matthew 7:6.

25   In *Nostradamus: Prophecies of Present Times?*, Aquarian Press, London, 1985.

26   There is, however, some evidence to suggest the Ancient Romans used lightning conductors to protect their buildings and it is just possible that Nostradamus may have known of this tradition.

27   Although some insist this refers to 1918, the year the Great War ended, not 1914, the year it began.

28   For a fuller discussion of this intriguing topic see, among other works, my *Occult Reich.*

29   Hitler has only got one ball/Goering has two, but they are small/Himmler has something similar/But poor old Goebbels has no balls at all!

30   Horbiger's notion that the universe was balanced in a conflict between eternal fire and eternal ice.

31   In the most recent at the time of writing, the Allied attack on Iraq following that country's annexation of Kuwait, more ordnance was expended in the first few days than in the whole of World War II.

32   Solidarity had, of course, the last laugh. At the time of writing, Walesa is President of Poland.

33   Quoted from *Nostradamus and the Millennium.*

34   Erika Cheetham makes a stab at linking it with the trouble the Holy Roman Empire had with the Turks.

35   I write in 1991, confident that the panic can only get worse.

36   Jonathan Cape Ltd, London, 1986.

37   *Good News from Outer Space*, Grafton Books, London, 1991.

38   There is support for the Far Eastern origin of this mysterious Oriental in Quatrain 54 of Century 5, which seems almost to duplicate the quatrain under consideration.

39   An American comedian joked recently that when Israel declared war on the Arabs in 1967, the Italian Army promptly surrendered.

40   In *Nostradamus: Prophecies of Present Times?*.

41   The back cover blurb to John Hogue's *Nostradamus and the Millennium* reads: 'The year 2000 approaches. Four hundred years ago the greatest prophet in history forecast the end of our world. The 20th Century closes with the Apocalypse . . . the Third World War . . . an end to the Catholic Church . . . a terrible Antichrist . . . Russia and America allied . . . New York under nuclear attack . . . Europe devastated . . . a new religious consciousness . . . a new age . . .'. One wonders why his publishers thought there was still time to make a profit on the book.

42   Alongside those we have already examined which tell of his magical methods of prophecy, there are various other 'occult' quatrains which may refer to alchemical processes, trance experience, astral projection and so on. There are even one or two which have the appearance of referring not to the future, but to the past, usually the Classical period of Greece or Rome.

43   While I have absolutely no ambition to revive the 'ancient astronauts' controversy which followed Erich Von Daniken's publication of *Chariots of the Gods?*, I cannot resist remarking that immortality or longevity are two of the most common characteristics traditionally attributed to 'gods'.

44   The death toll from the Bangladesh cyclone, current news as I write, is a stark reminder of how destructive nature can be.

45   The literal translation is 'Celtic people', a term Nostradamus frequently uses to refer to the French.

46   Elsewhere in the quatrains, Nostradamus suggests that some sort of control drug for AIDS will be developed fairly quickly, but an actual cure would take much longer.

47   I have to admit my translation here is also controversial. The original is 'Reb Roi' usually rendered as 'King Reb' and

sometimes related to the 'never-had-it-so-good' era of British Prime Minister Harold Macmillan. Since this in itself makes little sense, I have been tempted to suppose that Nostradamus misspelled or misheard the Scottish name.

48  *The Man Who Saw Tomorrow*, a title substantially better than the motion picture itself.

49  King of the Mongols almost certainly refers to Genghis Khan, who was born in 1167.

50  See *Genesis Revisited* by Zecharia Sitchin, Avon Books, New York, 1990.

# Index